Celebrate with a
Cake!

A step-by-step guide to creating 15 memorable cakes

LINDY SMITH

David & Charles

A DAVID & CHARLES BOOK
David & Charles is a subsidiary of F+W (UK) Ltd.,
an F+W Publications Inc. company

First published in the UK in 2005

Distributed in North America
by F+W Publications, Inc.
4700 East Galbraith Road
Cincinnati, OH 45236
1-800-289-0963

A catalogue record for this book is available from the
British Library.

ISBN 0 7153 1907 8 hardback
ISBN 0 7153 1845 4 paperback

Printed in China by SNP Leefung
for David & Charles
Brunel House   Newton Abbot   Devon

Commissioning Editor Fiona Eaton
Editor Jennifer Proverbs
Senior Designer Lisa Wyman
Production Controller Jen Campbell
Project Editor Jan Cutler
Photographer Karl Adamson

Visit our website at www.davidandcharles.co.uk

David & Charles books are available from all good
bookshops; alternatively you can contact our
Orderline on (0)1626 334555 or write to us at
FREEPOST EX2 110, David & Charles Direct, Newton
Abbot, TQ12 4ZZ (no stamp required UK mainland).

CONTENTS

Introduction

Designing and creating cakes is my passion, and one that I hope to share with you in the following pages. This book is a response to the many requests I have received from readers over the last few years. As well as weddings, birthdays and christenings, there are cakes for Valentine's Day, Mother's Day, a golden wedding anniversary and other celebrations, and they can all be adapted to suit other occasions. There is no limit to the inspirational ideas that you can copy and adapt.

Those of you who are familiar with my work will know that I love to be creative, and to break away from convention and try something new. I have included a wide range of cake shapes, including heart-shaped cakes, and even one that is shaped as a handbag and another as a teapot. Also included are column cakes and stacked columns, giving grand, sculptural shapes, which are perfect for celebrations. Some stunning cake separators have been used for the elegant display of multi-tiered cakes.

Various techniques can be found in the book, giving you the opportunity to achieve such effects as the gentle folds of fine fabric, delicate rose petals, soft, liquid swirls for decorative icing as well as modelling a gift-wrapped present, flowers, a baby, and a butterfly. You will also find exuberant ways of topping a celebration cake using feathers, hearts and flowers on fine wires.

To accompany the innovative cakes in the book there are also 'dress up' and 'dress down' ideas so that you can adapt the cakes according to your particular occasion, or make the designs simpler if you are new to cake decorating or more advanced if you are more experienced, or you may simply need a quicker version. There are also matching cup cake designs or variation ideas to go with each project. Most of the cakes are covered with sugarpaste (rolled fondant), but there are also buttercream-covered cakes, Exquisite Bouquet and Birthday Butterfly, for those who prefer them.

The cakes exhibit a variety of colours, and this is an area that can be particularly complex for the novice cake decorator. To help you to understand the way that colours work together I have included a detailed section on colour, which I hope will give you confidence to approach new colour schemes in your own designs.

If you're wondering where to gain inspiration for your cake designs, my own comes from the decorative paintings of Gustav Klimt (1862–1918), the colours used by the architect and designer, Charles Rennie Mackintosh (1868–1928), and the use of the scroll pattern in all decorative art forms. Observation and perception also play a large part in my designs – everything from the elegant to the quirky can provide creative inspiration.

How to use this book

Please read the reference section at the front of the book thoroughly; it explains how to begin tackling the cakes as well as some basic techniques. The projects use a variety of implements, and the most frequently used are listed in the Equipment List on pages 6–7. Where I have specified particular makes of cutters or decorations, I have added an abbreviation for the name of the supplier in brackets. You will find an abbreviations list with the Suppliers on page 104.

Recipes for the cakes, including baking times and quantities for various shapes, as well as all the different types of icing used in the book are provided. Cake Portions on page 10 will give you all the information you need to ensure that your cake will be large enough for the number of people you are providing for – you can add a tier to many of the cakes if you need to. To help you create the cakes, I have provided templates at the back of the book for projects where you will need to cut out a complicated shape. You will also find carving sketches for cakes that need to be intricately carved.

For a professional look you will need paste colours and dusts, and there are some good-quality decorations that you may wish to use to enhance your creation. These can be obtained from cake-decorating stores or by mail order; suppliers of equipment and ingredients can be found at the back of the book.

I hope you will feel inspired by the projects. Be adventurous – but most of all have fun and enjoy!

Lindy

email: lindy@lindyscakes.co.uk
website: www.lindyscakes.co.uk

Tackling Cakes

Although you will be keen to get started on one of the fantastic cake projects in this book, take a little time to read this section so that you are familiar with some of the important and basic points. This will help you to achieve good results.

Preparation

If your cake is to be a creation that you will be proud of, you will need to be fully prepared. Before you start your chosen project read through the instructions carefully so that you understand what is involved and how much time to allow. Make sure you have all the material and items of equipment to hand that you will need to complete the project.

Time planning

Try not to leave everything to the last minute, and plan your decorating time in advance. As the cakes baked from the recipes in this book last about two weeks, you have about one week to decorate the cake, leaving a week for it to be eaten.

Each project is split into stages to indicate natural breaks in the decorating process; for example, a simple two-stage project, such as the Floral Heart, could be carved and decorated over a two-day period. Some projects are obviously more involved than others, for example the Golden Wedding cake and Klimt Inspiration, so try to be realistic with what time you have available, and plan well in advance.

The Floral Heart cake can be made over two days.

Lining tins

It is quite simple to line cake tins (pans) well. Neatly lined tins will prevent the cake mixture from sticking and help to ensure a good shape.

1 Measure the circumference of your tin and cut a strip of baking parchment slightly longer than this measurement to allow for an overlap. Make the strip 5cm (2in) deeper than the height of the tin. Fold up 2.5cm (1in) along the bottom of the strip. For a round or heart-shaped tin, cut this fold with diagonal cuts. For a square, rectangular or hexagonal tin, crease the strip at intervals equal to the length of the inside edges of the tin, and then cut the folded section where it is creased into mitres (**A**).

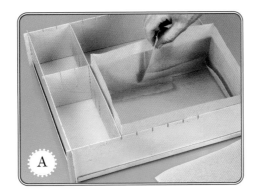

2 Grease the tin and place the strip around the side(s) with the cut edge on the base. Cut a piece of baking parchment to fit the base (**B**).

3 Care needs to be taken when lining ball tins. Cut two circles of the appropriate size from baking parchment:

♥ 15cm (6in) for a 10cm (4in) ball

♥ 20cm (8in) for a 13cm (5in) ball

♥ 25.5cm (10in) for a 15cm (6in) ball

4 Fold the circles into quarters to find their centres. Open out the circles and make radial cuts into the circle (**C**). Grease both the tin and one side of the paper and place the circle into the centre of one half of the tin, greased sides together. Encourage the paper to fit the tin by overlapping the sections.

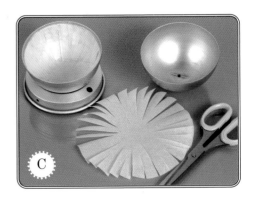

Equipment List

The following is a list of items of equipment that have been frequently used in the book. There are many other sugarcraft items available that you can experiment with. Details can be obtained from the suppliers listed at the back of the book.

CAKE BOARDS
★ Drum, a thick board used to display the cakes (1).

★ Hardboard, a thin, strong board used in the construction of stacked cakes (2).

CELPAD (CC), a surface on which to thin flower petals (3).

COCKTAIL STICK (toothpick) used as a marker and to transfer small amounts of paste colour (4).

CRAFT KNIFE for intricate cutting tasks (5).

CUTTERS
★ Circle (plastic, and small and large metal), for cutting modelling paste (6).

★ Heart, for indenting paste on the Valentine cup cakes (not shown).

★ Shield (FMM), for cutting out the doorways on Fairytale Castle (not shown).

★ Blossom plunger set (PME), to create small flowers, as on Pink Sparkle (7).

★ Large blossom (FMM) used for the flowers on Floral Heart (8).

★ Daisy collection (FMM), for making daisies, as for Stylish Handbag and the Floral Heart (9).

★ Large strawberry calyx (JEM), for cutting the groom's hair on Pink Sparkle (10).

★ Leaf hearts (T), used as templates and cutters on the Golden Wedding cake (11).

★ Squares, used on Klimt Inspiration (not shown).

★ Long teardrop, used on Klimt Inspiration (12).

★ Set of triangles, for the ball decoration on Klimt Inspiration (13).

★ Diamonds, used to cut castle windows on Fairytale Castle (not shown).

★ No. 4 straight frill (FMM), used for the parapet of the Fairytale Castle (14).

★ Micro daisy (CC), used on the Floral Heart (15).

★ Toy tappits (FMM), used on the Christening Gift (16).

DOWEL (W) used to support cakes and make them stable (17).

MEASURING SPOONS for accurate measuring of ingredients (18).

MOULDS
★ Baby Head mould (HP), for creating a realistic baby face, as on Baby's Blanket (19).

★ Daisy centre mould (JEM), for creating realistic daisy centres, as on Stylish Handbag (20).

MULTI-RIBBON CUTTER (FMM) time-saving tool for cutting even strips of paste (21).

OASIS FIX a florists' adhesive for securing wires into the posy pick (22).

PAINTBRUSHES (including stippling brush) a range of sizes is useful for painting and dusting (23).

PALETTE KNIFE used for cutting paste (24).

PATCHWORK CUTTERS used to emboss and cut out paste:
★ Poppy, used on Time for Tea (25).

★ Patchwork set, used on Baby's Blanket (26).

★ Make a Cradle, used on Baby's Blanket and Christening Gift (27).

PIN (glass-headed) used to hold templates temporarily in position (28).

PIPING TUBES (TIPS) for piping buttercream and royal icing, and for cutting out small circles (29).

POSY PICK for inserting into cakes to hold wires (30).

REUSABLE PIPING BAG AND COUPLER to hold buttercream or royal icing whilst piping. The coupler is connected to the piping bag and allows the tube to be changed easily (31).

ROLLING PINS for rolling out the different types of paste (32).

SCISSORS for cutting templates and trimming paste to shape (33).

SET SQUARE for accurate alignment (34).

SMOOTHER helps to create a smooth and even finish to sugarpaste (35).

SPACERS narrow and 5mm (³⁄₁₆in) for rolling out paste (36).

SPIRIT LEVEL to check dowels are vertical and that the tops of cakes are horizontal (37).

SUGAR SHAPER AND DISCS to create pieces of uniformly shaped modelling paste (38).

TINS (pans) small and medium ball, multisized square and multisized round for baking cakes (39).

TOOLS

★ Ball tool, makes even indentations in paste and softens the edges of petals (40).

★ Dresden tool, to create markings on paste (41).

★ Cutting wheel, used instead of a knife to avoid dragging the paste (42).

★ 'U' tool, used to open mouths for realistic faces (43).

WORK BOARD non-stick, used for rolling out pastes (44).

PIPING TUBES
The following piping tubes have been used in the book. As tube numbers may vary with different suppliers, always check the tube diameter:

TUBE NO.	DIAMETER
1	1mm (¹⁄₃₂in)
2	1.5mm (¹⁄₁₆in)
3	2mm (³⁄₃₂in)
4	3mm (³⁄₃₂in)
16	5mm (³⁄₁₆in)
17	6mm (¼in)
18	7mm (⁹⁄₃₂)

Baking Cakes

Madeira cake

A firm, moist cake, Madeira will keep for up to two weeks. I allow one week to decorate it and one for it to be eaten. See facing page for the recipe.

1 Preheat the oven to 160°C/325°F/Gas 3. Grease and line the cake tin (pan) with baking parchment (see page 5).

2 Cream the butter and sugar in a large mixing bowl until light, fluffy and pale. Sift the flours together in a separate bowl.

3 Beat the eggs into the creamed mixture, one at a time, following each with a spoonful of flour, to prevent the mixture curdling.

4 Sift the remaining flour into the creamed mixture and fold in carefully with a large metal spoon. Add the flavouring, if using.

5 Transfer to the lined bakeware and bake for the time given. When the cake is ready it will be well risen, firm to the touch and a skewer inserted into the centre will come out clean.

6 Leave the cake to cool in the tin then, leaving the lining paper on, wrap the cake in foil or place in an airtight container for at least 12 hours before cutting, to allow the cake to settle.

FLAVOURINGS
Traditionally, Madeira cake was flavoured with lemon, but it can also be made with other flavourings (flavourings are given for a six-egg quantity Madeira cake; increase or decrease the amounts for other quantities):

★**Lemon**: grated rind of 2 lemons

★**Vanilla**: 5ml (1 tsp) vanilla extract

★**Cherry**: 350g (12oz) glacé (candied) cherries, halved

★**Fruit**: 350g (12oz) sultanas (golden raisins), currants, raisins or dates

★**Coconut**: 110g (3¾oz) desiccated (dry unsweetened shredded) coconut

★**Almond**: 5ml (1 tsp) almond essence (extract) and 45ml (3 tbsp) ground almonds

Chocolate cake

This is a rich, moist, yet firm, chocolate cake. The secret to success is to use good quality chocolate with a reasonably high cocoa solids content; for example, luxury plain Belgian chocolate with a cocoa solids content of around 50 per cent works well. See facing page for the recipe.

1 Preheat the oven to 180°C/350°F/Gas 4. Grease and line the cake tin (pan) with baking parchment (see page 5).

2 Melt the chocolate, either in a double boiler or in a microwave. Cream the butter and sugar in a large mixing bowl until light, fluffy and pale.

3 Separate the eggs. Gradually add the egg yolks, then the melted chocolate. In a separate bowl, whisk the egg whites to soft peaks. Gradually whisk the icing sugar into the egg whites.

4 Sift the flour into another bowl and, using a large metal spoon, fold the flour alternately with the egg whites into the chocolate mixture.

5 Transfer the mixture into the lined bakeware, and bake. Baking times will depend on your oven, the cake tin used and the depth of the cake. I usually check small cakes after 30 minutes, medium-sized cakes after an hour, and large cakes after 2 hours. When the cake is baked it will be well risen, firm to the touch and a skewer inserted into the centre will come out clean.

6 Allow the cake to cool completely in the tin, then, leaving the lining paper on, wrap the cake in foil or place in an airtight container for at least 12 hours before cutting to allow the cake to settle.

Cup cakes

Ready-made cup cakes are useful and quick when you are short of time, but home-made taste better. See facing page for the recipe.

1 Preheat the oven to 160°C/325°F/Gas 3 and line bun trays with fluted paper baking cases. Prepare the Madeira cake mixture (see steps 1–4 of Madeira cake recipe, left).

2 Fill each paper case half-full. Bake for approximately 20 minutes.

3 Let the cakes stand in the trays for 5 minutes before transferring to a rack to cool completely.

Carefully break each egg into a cup to prevent small pieces of eggshell falling into the batter.

USING A BALL TIN
How you bake your cake in a ball tin (pan) depends on the type of cake:

Fruit cake
Pile the mixture into the lower half of the tin, creating a dome, the height of which should be about 1–2cm (⅜–¾in) from the top of the tin when it is assembled. This small space allows the mixture to rise and fill the tin whilst baking.

Sponge cake
Bake sponge cake balls in two halves. Allow the halves to cool in the tin then level each cake using the edge of the tin, see levelling cakes page 14, and stick the two halves together to create a perfect sphere.

Madeira Cake Quantities

CAKE SIZES		UNSALTED BUTTER (sweet butter)	CASTER SUGAR (superfine sugar)	SELF-RAISING FLOUR (self-rising flour)	PLAIN FLOUR (all-purpose flour)	EGGS (large) (US extra large)	BAKING TIMES at 160°C/ 325°F/Gas 3
10cm (4in) round/ball		75g (3oz)	75g (3oz)	75g (3oz)	40g (1½oz)	1	¾–1 hour
13cm (5in) round	10cm (4in) square	115g (4oz)	115g (4oz)	115g (4oz)	50g (2oz)	2	¾–1 hour
15cm (6in) round/ petal/hexagonal	36 cup cake cases/ 13cm (5in) square/ball	175g (6oz)	175g (6oz)	175g (6oz)	75g (3oz)	3	1–1¼ hours
18cm (7in) round	15cm (6in) square	225g (8oz)	225g (8oz)	225g (8oz)	115g (4oz)	4	1–1¼ hours
20cm (8in) round/heart	18cm (7in) square	350g (12oz)	350g (12oz)	350g (12oz)	175g (6oz)	6	1¼–1½ hours
23cm (9in) round	20cm (8in) square	450g (1lb)	450g (1lb)	450g (1lb)	225g (8oz)	8	1½–1¾ hours
25.5cm (10in) round/hexagonal	23cm (9in) square	500g (1lb 2oz)	500g (1lb 2oz)	500g (1lb 2oz)	250g (9oz)	9	1½–1¾ hours
30cm (12in) round	28cm (11in) square	850g (1lb 14oz)	850g (1lb 14oz)	850g (1lb 14oz)	425g (15oz)	15	2–2¼ hours

Chocolate Cake Quantities

CAKE SIZES	PLAIN CHOCOLATE (semi-sweet chocolate)	UNSALTED BUTTER (sweet butter)	CASTER SUGAR (superfine sugar)	EGGS (large) (US extra large)	ICING SUGAR (confectioners' sugar)	SELF-RAISING FLOUR (self-rising flour)	BAKING TIMES at 180°C/ 350°F/Gas 4
10cm (4in) round/ball	75g (3oz)	50g (2oz)	40g (1½oz)	2	15g (½oz)	40g (1½oz)	30–45 mins
13cm (5in) round 10cm (4in) square	125g (4½oz)	75g (3oz)	50g (2oz)	3	20g (¾oz)	75g (3oz)	45 mins–1 hour
15cm (6in) round/ hexagonal/petal 13cm (5in) square/ball	175g (6oz)	115g (4oz)	75g (3oz)	4	25g (1oz)	115g (4oz)	45 mins–1 hour
18cm (7in) round 15cm (6in) square	225g (8oz)	175g (6oz)	115g (4oz)	6	40g (1½oz)	175g (6oz)	1–1¼ hours
20cm (8in) round/heart 18cm (7in) square	275g (10oz)	225g (8oz)	150g (5oz)	8	50g (2oz)	225g (8oz)	1–1¼ hours
23cm (9in) round/ 20cm (8in) square	425g (15oz)	275g (10oz)	175g (6oz)	10	70g (2½oz)	275g (10oz)	1¼–1½ hours
25.5cm (10in) round 23cm (9in) square	500g (1lb 2oz)	350g (12oz)	225g (8oz)	12	75g (3oz)	350g (12oz)	1½–1¾ hours
30cm (12in) round 28cm (11in) square	875g (1lb 15oz)	550g (1¼lb)	375g (13oz)	20	125g (4½oz)	550g (¼lb)	2–2¼ hours

Cake Portions

The number of portions cut from a cake depends on whether the cake cuts cleanly and the dexterity of the person cutting the cake.

The fruit cake portions on the chart have been based on 2.5cm (1in) square slices but many caterers do cut smaller than this, so your cake will go a lot further. However, it is always better to overestimate the number of portions required. Sponge cakes are served in larger portions, 5 x 2.5cm (2 x 1in), at least double the size of fruit cake slices.

Allow extra cake if you want larger portions for, say, a tea-time birthday cake.

CAKE SIZES		APPROXIMATE PORTIONS	
		Fruit cake 2.5cm (1in) square slices	Sponge cake 5 x 2.5cm (2 x 1in) slices
10cm (4in) round/ball		12	6
13cm (5in) round	10cm (4in) square	16	8
15cm (6in) round/hexagonal/petal	13cm (5in) square/ball	24	12
18cm (7in) round	15cm (6in) square	34	17
20cm (8in) round/heart	18cm (7in) square	46	23
23cm (9in) round	20cm (8in) square	58	29
25.5cm (10in) round	23cm (9in) square	70	35
30cm (12in) round	28cm (11in) square	100	50

Adapting a Favourite Recipe

If you have a favourite recipe that you would like to use for one of the cakes in the book then just refer to the chart below and adapt it accordingly.

How to use the chart: the chart assumes that your own basic recipe will be for a 20cm (8in) round cake, as this is the most common size. Therefore, if you want to make a 25.5cm (10in) round cake, for example, look at the chart and you will see that you need 1½ times the quantity of your usual recipe.

CAKE SIZES			MULTIPLES OF YOUR OWN BASIC RECIPE
Round, hexagonal, petal and heart	Square	Ball	(approximate quantities)
10cm (4in)		10cm (4in)	¼
13cm (5in)	10cm (4in)		⅓
15cm (6in)	13cm (5in)	13cm (5in)	½
18cm (7in)	15cm (6in)		¾
20cm (8in)	18cm (7in)	15cm (6in)	1
23cm (9in)	20cm (8in)		1¼
25.5cm (10in)	23cm (9in)		1½
28cm (11in)	25.5cm (10in)		2
30cm (12in)	28cm (11in)		2½
33cm (13in)	30cm (12in)		3

If you wish to use a tin (pan) that is not mentioned above, such as a pre-formed shaped tin or oval, fill a 20cm (8in) tin with water and compare it with the quantity of water that your tin holds. The basic recipe quantity can then be multiplied or divided as necessary.

Fruit cake

1 Soak the sultanas, currants, raisins and chopped peal in brandy overnight.

2 Preheat the oven to 150°C/300°F/Gas 2. Sieve the flour, spice and ground almonds into a bowl. In another bowl cream the butter and sugar until light, fluffy and pale. Do not overbeat.

3 Lightly mix together the eggs, treacle and vanilla, beat into the creamed mixture a little at a time adding a spoonful of flour after each addition.

4 Rinse the cherries and chop, add to the fruit with the lemon rind and juice, chopped almonds and a small amount of flour. Fold the remaining flour into the creamed mixture, followed by the dried fruit. Add extra brandy or milk if necessary.

5 Spoon into a lined cake tin (pan), level the top, and then slightly hollow the centre.Tie a double layer of brown paper or newspaper around the outside of the tin to protect the cake during cooking, and place a container of water in the oven to help keep your cake moist.

6 Bake at 150°C/300°F/Gas 2 for the stated cooking time and then reduce the temperature to 120°C/250°F/Gas ½ and bake further for the time suggested. When the cake is baked it will be firm to the touch and a skewer inserted into the centre will come out clean. Allow the cake to cool in the tin.

You can add extra brandy to the cake while it is still cooling if you like. Prick the surface all over with a skewer and spoon some brandy over.

7 Leaving the lining paper on, wrap the cake in baking parchment and then foil. Never store your cake in foil only, as the acid in the fruit will attack the foil. Store the cake in a cool, dry place. Fruit cake should be aged for at least one month to allow the flavour to mature. Wedding cakes are traditionally stored for at least three months to give them a nicely matured flavour and to enable the cake to be cut cleanly into small portions. (Fruit cake that is not mature will be just as delicious, but difficult to cut neatly. Although fine for a family birthday, it would not be suitable for a wedding.)

Fruit Cake Quantities

	10CM (4IN) ROUND/BALL	13CM (5IN) ROUND 10CM (4IN) SQUARE	15CM (6IN) ROUND/PETAL 13CM (5IN) SQUARE/BALL	18CM (7IN) ROUND 15CM (6IN) SQUARE	20CM (8IN) ROUND/HEART 18CM (7IN) SQUARE	23CM (9IN) ROUND 20CM (8IN) SQUARE	25.5CM(10IN) ROUND/ HEXAGONAL 23CM (9IN) SQUARE	30CM (12IN) ROUND 28CM (11IN) SQUARE
sultanas (golden raisins)	50g (2oz)	75g (3oz)	115g (4oz)	175g (6oz)	225g (8oz)	275g (10oz)	350g (12oz)	550g (1¼lb)
currants	50g (2oz)	75g (3oz)	115g (4oz)	175g (6oz)	225g (8oz)	275g (10oz)	350g (12oz)	550g (1¼lb)
raisins	50g (2oz)	75g (3oz)	115g (4oz)	175g (6oz)	225g (8oz)	275g (10oz)	350g (12oz)	550g (1¼lb)
chopped peal	25g (1oz)	40g (1½oz)	50g (2oz)	75g (3oz)	115g (4oz)	150g (5oz)	175g (6oz)	275g (10oz)
brandy	7.5ml (1½ tsp)	11.5ml (2¼ tsp)	15ml (1 tbsp)	25ml (1½ tbsp)	30ml (2 tbsp)	37.5ml (2½ tbsp)	45ml (3 tbsp)	75ml (5 tbsp)
plain flour (all-purpose)	50g (2oz)	75g (3oz)	115g (4oz)	175g (6oz)	225g (8oz)	275g (10oz)	350g (12oz)	550g (1¼lb)
mixed spice (apple pie)	1.5ml (¼ tsp)	2.5ml (½ tsp)	2.5ml (½ tsp)	3.5ml (¾ tsp)	5ml (1 tsp)	6.5ml (1¼tsp)	7.5ml (1½ tsp)	12.5ml (2½ tsp)
ground almonds	15g (½oz)	20g (¾oz)	25g (1oz)	40g (1½oz)	50g (2oz)	70g (2½oz)	75g (3oz)	150g (5oz)
butter	50g (2oz)	75g (3oz)	115g (4oz)	175g (6oz)	225g (8oz)	275g (10oz)	350g (12oz)	550g (1¼lb)
soft brown sugar	50g (2oz)	75g (3oz)	115g (4oz)	175g (6oz)	225g (8oz)	275g (10oz)	350g (12oz)	550g (1¼lb)
eggs	1	1½	2	3	4	5	6	10
black treacle	2.5ml (½ tsp)	5ml (1 tsp)	7.5ml (1½ tsp)	15ml (1 tbsp)	15ml (1 tbsp)	20ml (4 tsp)	25ml (1½ tbsp)	37.5ml (2½ tbsp)
vanilla extract	a few drops	1.5ml (¼ tsp)	1.5ml (¼ tsp)	2.5ml (½ tsp)	2.5ml (½ tsp)	3.5ml (¾ tsp)	3.5ml (¾ tsp)	6.5ml (1¼ tsp)
glacé (candied) cherries	25g (1oz)	40g (1½oz)	50g (2oz)	75g (3oz)	115g (4oz)	150g (5oz)	175g (6oz)	275g (10oz)
lemon rind and juice	¼ lemon	⅓ lemon	½ lemon	¾ lemon	1 lemon	1¼ lemons	1½ lemons	2½ lemons
chopped almonds	15g (½oz)	20g (¾oz)	25g (1oz)	40g (1½oz)	50g (2oz)	70g (2½oz)	75g (3oz)	150g (5oz)
cooking times (approx.) 150°C/300°F/Gas 2	30 minutes	30 minutes	50 minutes	1 hour	1½ hours	1¾ hours	2 hours	2½ hours
120°C/250°F/Gas ½	30 minutes	1 hour	1 hour 40 minutes	2¼ hours	2½ hours	3¼ hours	4 hours	5½ hours
total	1 hour	1½ hours	2½ hours	3¼ hours	4 hours	5 hours	6 hours	8 hours

Sugar Recipes

Most of the sugar recipes used in the book for covering, modelling and decoration can easily be made at home. Use paste colours to colour them according to the individual project.

Sugarpaste

Ready-made sugarpaste (rolled fondant) can be obtained from supermarkets and cake-decorating suppliers, and is available in white and the whole colour spectrum. It is also easy and inexpensive to make your own.

Ingredients Makes 1kg (2¼lb)
- 60ml (4 tbsp) cold water
- 20ml (4 tsp/1 sachet) powdered gelatine
- 125ml (4fl oz) liquid glucose
- 15ml (1 tbsp) glycerine
- 1kg (2¼lb) icing (confectioners') sugar, sieved, plus extra for dusting

1 Place the water in a small bowl, sprinkle over the gelatine and soak until spongy. Stand the bowl over a pan of hot but not boiling water and stir until the gelatine is dissolved. Add the glucose and glycerine, stirring until well blended and runny.

2 Put the icing sugar in a large bowl. Make a well in the centre and slowly pour in the liquid ingredients, stirring constantly. Mix well. Turn out on to a surface dusted with icing sugar and knead until smooth, sprinkling with extra icing sugar if the paste becomes too sticky. The paste can be used immediately or tightly wrapped and stored in a plastic bag until required.

Pastillage

This is an extremely useful paste because, unlike modelling paste, it sets extremely hard and is not affected by moisture the way other pastes are. However, the paste crusts quickly and is brittle once dry. You can buy it in a powdered form, to which you add water, but it is easy to make yourself.

Ingredients Makes 350g (12oz)
- 1 egg white
- 300g (11oz) icing (confectioners') sugar, sifted
- 10ml (2 tsp) gum tragacanth

1 Put the egg white into a large mixing bowl. Gradually add enough icing sugar until the mixture combines together into a ball. Mix in the gum tragacanth, and then turn the paste out on to a work board or work surface and knead the pastillage well.

2 Incorporate the remaining icing sugar into the remainder of pastillage to give a stiff paste. Store pastillage in a polythene bag placed in an airtight container in a refrigerator for up to one month.

Modelling paste

This versatile paste keeps its shape well, dries harder than sugarpaste and is used throughout the book for adding detail to covered cakes. Although there are commercial pastes available, it is easy and a lot cheaper to make your own.

Ingredients Makes 225g (8oz)
- 225g (8oz) sugarpaste (rolled fondant)
- 5ml (1 tsp) gum tragacanth

Make a well in the sugarpaste and add the gum tragacanth. Knead in. Wrap in a plastic bag and allow the gum to work before use. You will begin to feel a difference in the paste after an hour or so, but it is best left overnight. The modelling paste should be firm but pliable with a slight elastic texture. Kneading the modelling paste makes it warm and easy to work with.

Modelling-paste tips
- Gum tragacanth is a natural gum available from cake-decorating suppliers.
- If time is short use CMC instead of gum tragacanth; this is a synthetic product but it works almost straight away.
- Placing your modelling paste in a microwave for a few seconds is an excellent way of warming it for use.
- If you have previously added a large amount of colour to your paste and it is consequently too soft, an extra pinch or two of gum tragacanth will be necessary.
- If your paste is crumbly or too hard to work, add a touch of white vegetable fat (shortening) and a little boiled water, and knead until softened.

Sugar glue

Although commercially available, sugar glue is quick and easy to make at home.

Break up pieces of white modelling paste into a small container and cover with boiling water. Stir until dissolved. This produces a thick, strong glue, which can be easily thinned by adding some more cooled boiled water. If a strong glue is required, use pastillage rather than modelling paste as the base (useful for delicate work, but not needed for any projects in this book).

Buttercream

Used to sandwich cakes together, to coat them before covering with sugarpaste or on its own as a cake covering.

Ingredients Makes 1 quantity

- 110g (3¾oz) unsalted (sweet) butter
- 350g (12oz) icing (confectioners') sugar
- 15–30ml (1–2 tbsp) milk or water
- a few drops of vanilla extract or alternative flavouring

Place the butter in a bowl and beat until light and fluffy. Sift the icing sugar into the bowl and continue to beat until the mixture changes colour. Add just enough milk or water to give a firm but spreadable consistency. Flavour by adding the vanilla or alternative flavouring, then store the buttercream in an airtight container until required.

White buttercream

An alternative for those on a dairy-free diet, this is used for coating Exquisite Bouquet. Simply follow the buttercream recipe but replace the butter with solid white vegetable fat (shortening).

Chocolate buttercream

To make chocolate buttercream, follow the buttercream recipe above and mix 30ml (2 tbsp) of unsweetened cocoa powder with the milk or water before adding it to the butter and sugar mixture. Omit the flavourings.

White chocolate buttercream

Ingredients Makes 1 quantity

- 115g (4oz) white chocolate
- 115g (4oz) unsalted (sweet) butter
- 225g (8oz) icing sugar

Melt the chocolate in a bowl over hot water and leave to cool slightly. Soften the butter and beat in the sugar, and then beat in the chocolate.

Confectioners' glaze

Used to add a realistic gloss to the eyes of figures and where a glossy-looking sheen is needed, such as on the Valentine Romance board, confectioners' glaze is available from cake-decorating suppliers.

White vegetable fat

This is a solid white vegetable fat (shortening) that is often known by a brand name: in the UK, Trex or White Flora; in South Africa, Holsum; in Australia, Copha; and in America, Crisco. These products are more or less interchangeable in cake making.

Flowerpaste (petal/gum paste)

Available commercially from sugarcraft suppliers, flowerpaste can be bought in white and a variety of colours. There are many varieties available so try a few to see which you prefer. Alternatively, it is possible to make your own, but it is a time-consuming process and you will need a heavy-duty mixer.

Ingredients Makes 500g (1lb 2oz)

- 500g (1lb 2oz) icing (confectioners') sugar
- 15ml (1 tbsp) gum tragacanth
- 25ml (1½ tbsp) cold water
- 10ml (2 tsp) powered gelatine
- 10ml (2 tsp) liquid glucose
- 15ml (1 tbsp) white vegetable fat (shortening)
- 1 medium egg white

1 Sieve the icing sugar and gum tragacanth into the greased mixing bowl of a heavy-duty mixer (the grease eases the strain on the machine).

2 Place the water in a small bowl, sprinkle over the gelatine and soak until spongy. Stand the bowl over a pan of hot but not boiling water and stir until the gelatine is dissolved. Add the glucose and white fat to the gelatine and continue heating until all the ingredients are melted and mixed.

3 Add the glucose mixture and egg white to the icing sugar. Beat the mixture very slowly until mixed – at this stage it will be a beige colour – then increase the speed to maximum until the paste becomes white and stringy.

4 Grease your hands and remove the paste from the bowl. Pull and stretch the paste several times, and then knead together. Place in a plastic bag and store in an airtight container. Leave the paste to mature for at least 12 hours.

Using flowerpaste

Flowerpaste dries quickly, so when using cut off only as much as you need and reseal the remainder. Work it well with your fingers, it should 'click' between your fingers when it is ready to use. If it is too hard and crumbly, add a little egg white and white vegetable fat – the fat slows down the drying process and the egg white makes it more pliable.

Royal icing

Use royal icing to pipe fine detail.

Ingredients Makes 1 quantity

- 1 egg white
- 250g (9oz) icing (confectioners') sugar, sifted

Put the egg white in a bowl and gradually beat in the icing sugar until the icing is glossy and forms soft peaks.

Covering Cakes and Boards

Follow these basic techniques to achieve a neat and professional appearance to the initial cake and board coverings. With care and practice you will soon find that you have a perfectly smooth finish.

Levelling the cake

Making an accurate cake base is an important part of creating your masterpiece. There are two ways to do this, depending on the cake:

1 Place a set square up against the edge of the cake and, with a sharp knife, mark a line around the top of the cake at the required height: 7–7.5cm (2¾–3in) for the cakes in this book. With a large serrated knife cut around the marked line and across the cake to remove the domed crust.

2 Place a cake board into the base of the tin (pan) in which the cake was baked so that when the cake is placed on top, the outer edge of the cake will be level with the tin, and the dome will protrude above. Take a long, sharp knife and cut the dome from the cake, keeping the knife against the tin. This will ensure the cake is completely level (**A**).

For perfect results, use a knife that is wider than the tin.

Apricot glaze

This glaze is traditionally used to stick marzipan to fruit cakes. You can also use other jams or jellies, such as apple jelly. Redcurrant jelly is delicious on chocolate cakes when a marzipan covering is used.

Place 115g (4oz) apricot jam and 30ml (2 tbsp) of water into a pan. Heat gently until the jam has melted, and then boil rapidly for 30 seconds. Strain through a sieve, if pieces of fruit are present. Use warm.

Covering a cake with marzipan

A fruit cake should be covered with marzipan before the sugarpaste covering is applied, to add flavour, to seal in the moisture and to prevent the fruit staining the sugarpaste.

1 Unwrap the cake and roll over the top with a rolling pin to flatten it slightly. Turn the cake over so that the flatter surface (the base), becomes the top, and place on waxed paper.

2 Knead the marzipan so that it becomes supple; do not over-knead as this releases oils from the marzipan and changes its consistency.

3 Brush apricot glaze into the gap around the base of the cake. Roll a long sausage of marzipan and place it around the base of the cake (**B**), press it under the cake with the help of a smoother, to fill any gaps (**C**).

4 Brush the cake with warm apricot glaze and use small pieces of marzipan to fill any holes in the cake. Roll out the marzipan between some 5mm (³⁄₁₆in) spacers, using icing (confectioners') sugar or white vegetable fat (shortening) to stop it sticking to your work board or work surface. Turn the marzipan around whilst rolling to maintain an appropriate shape, but do not turn the marzipan over.

5 Lift up the marzipan over a rolling pin and place over the cake (**D**). Smooth the top of the cake with a smoother to remove any air bubbles, and then gently ease the marzipan down the sides of the cake into position, making sure there are no pleats. Smooth the top curved edge with the palm of your hand and the sides with a smoother.

6 Gradually press down with the smoother around the edge of the cake into the excess marzipan, and then trim this away to create a neat edge (**E**). It is advisable to allow the marzipan to harden in a warm, dry place for 24–48 hours to give a firmer base before decorating.

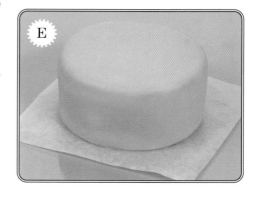

Marzipan tips

♥ Choose a white marzipan with a smooth texture and high almond content (at least 23.5 per cent).

♥ Check you are not using icing (confectioners') sugar with added cornflour (cornstarch) to roll out your marzipan as the presence of cornflour may cause fermentation.

CAKE SIZES		MARZIPAN QUANTITIES 5MM (³⁄₁₆IN) THICKNESS
10cm (4in) round/ball		350g (12oz)
13cm (5in) round	10cm (4in) square	425g (15oz)
15cm (6in) round/ hexagonal/petal	13cm (5in) square/ball	500g (1lb 2oz)
18cm (7in) round	15cm (6in) square	750g (1lb 10oz)
20cm (8in) round/heart	18cm (7in) square	900g (2lb)
23cm (9in) round	20cm (8in) square	1kg (2¼lb)
25.5cm (10in) round	23cm (9in) square	1.25kg (2¾lb)
30cm (12in) round	28cm (11in) square	1.75kg (3¾lb)

Applying a sugarpaste covering

For a fruit cake, moisten the surface of the marzipan with clear spirit, such as gin or vodka. Form an even coating; if you leave dry patches, air bubbles may form under the sugarpaste (rolled fondant).

For a sponge cake, prepare the cake by covering it with a thin layer of buttercream to fill in any holes and help the sugarpaste stick to the surface.

1 Knead the sugarpaste until warm and pliable. Roll out on a surface lightly dusted with icing (confectioners') sugar, or if you have a large corian work board or work surface use white vegetable fat (shortening) instead. White fat works well, and you don't have the problems of icing sugar drying out or marking the sugarpaste. Roll the paste to a depth of 5mm (³⁄₁₆in). It is a good idea to use spacers for this, as they ensure an even thickness (**F**).

2 Lift the paste carefully over the top of the cake, supporting it with a rolling pin, and position it so that it covers the cake (**G**). Smooth the surface of the cake to remove any lumps and bumps using a smoother for the flat areas and a combination of smoother and the palm of your hand for the curved ones (**H**). Always make sure your hands are clean and dry with no traces of icing sugar before smoothing sugarpaste.

3 Trim away the excess paste with a palette knife (**I**); it often helps to make a cutting line with a smoother, by pressing the smoother down around the edge of the cake into the excess paste before you trim it.

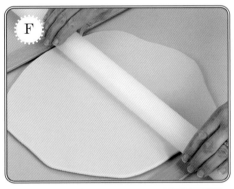

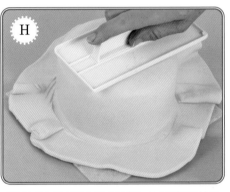

If you find you have unwanted air bubbles under the icing, insert a clean glass-headed dressmakers' pin at an angle and press out the air.

Covering boards

Roll out the sugarpaste to a depth of 4mm (⅛in), ideally using spacers. Moisten the board with water or sugar glue. Lift up the paste and drape over the board. Circle a smoother over the paste to achieve a smooth, flat finish to the board. Cut the paste flush with the sides of the board, taking care to keep the edge vertical. The covered board should then be left overnight to dry thoroughly.

Assembling Multi-tiered Cakes

A multi-tiered cake, like a building, needs a structure hidden within it to prevent it from collapsing. It is important that this structure is 'built' correctly to take the loads put upon it, so please follow the instructions carefully, as it is worth the time involved to get this stage correct.

Dowelling cakes

All but the top cake will usually need dowelling to provide support.

1 To dowel a cake, centre a cake board the same size as the tier above (or the size of the cake separator base plate, if dowelling for a separator) and scribe around the edge of the board (**A**) to leave a visible outline.

2 Insert a wooden dowel 2.5cm (1in) in from the scribed line vertically down through the cake to the cake board below. Make a knife scratch or pencil mark on the dowel to mark the exact height and remove the dowel (**B**).

3 Tape four dowels together. Then, using the mark on the inserted dowel, draw a pencil cutting line over the tape on the four dowels, making sure that the line is 90 degrees to the dowels (a set square helps) (**C**). Next, using a small saw, such as a mitre saw that holds the dowels firm as it cuts, saw across the dowels.

4 Place one of the dowels back in the measuring hole and insert the other dowels vertically down to the cake board at 3, 6 and 9 o'clock to the first one (**D**).

5 Repeat steps 1–4 for all but the top cake.

It is essential that all the dowels are inserted vertically, are all the same length and have flat tops.

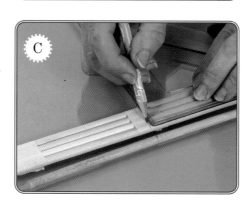

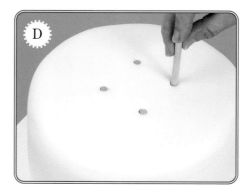

Stacking cakes

Column cakes: These are dowelled and stacked before being covered with icing (see Exquisite Bouquet, page 94).

Cover the top of the cakes, with the exception of the top tier, with buttercream or apricot glaze, as appropriate for the type of cake being used. Then place the cakes directly on top of one another, ensuring that their sides are vertical.

Covered cakes: Each cake is covered with icing and dowelled before it is stacked (see Fun Flowers, page 82). Place 15ml (1 tbsp) royal icing within the scribed area of the base cake and stack the next sized cake on top using the scribed line as a placement guide. Repeat the same process with the remaining cakes.

Exquisite Bouquet, page 94

Using cake separators

Traditionally, pillars have been used to separate one tier from another. However, stylish and elegant metalwork cake separators are now available, as shown.

1 Dowel the cake that the separator will rest on under the area of the base plate. Stick a thin cake card to the base of the separator using royal icing (**E**). (This acts as a barrier, as the separator should not come into contact with the cake.)

2 Position the cake separator on the dowelled cake using royal icing to secure. Leave the royal icing to set.

3 Once the icing has set, place a cake on the top plate and secure in place, for example by using non-slip matting (**F**) or a little oasis fix.

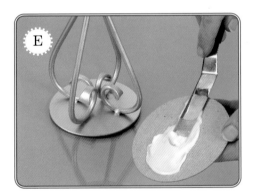

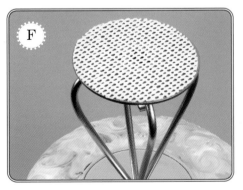

Golden Wedding, page 58 (above) and the Klimt Inspiration variation, page 81 (right)

Decorating and Storage

You can experiment with a variety of decorations available to the sugarcrafter to enhance your cakes. Store your final creation carefully to ensure that it remains in perfect condition before it is served.

Edible decorations

There is an ever-increasing variety of ready-made decorations available from supermarkets and sugarcraft suppliers, and they are a great way of saving time and adding that extra touch when used wisely. Dragées (sugar balls) are particularly attractive and are used on a number of projects in this book as they add a touch of glamour and opulence to the cakes, such as the Art Deco Feathers.

Non-edible decorations

The use of non-edible decorations is becoming popular on celebration cakes. You can go to town with your decoration ideas and include feathers, all kinds of wires and a myriad of beads. Look at the work of florists, jewellery makers and interior designers to give you inspiration. Always remember that non-edible beads should not be stuck to the sides of the cake and that wires should be inserted into a posy pick and never directly into a cake.

Storage

Protect your cake by placing it in a clean, covered cake box, and store somewhere cool and dry, but never in a refrigerator. If the box is slightly larger than the cake and the cake is to be transported, use non-slip matting to prevent the cake moving.

Modelling-paste models can be kept forever if placed in a dry, sealed case and stored in the dark. They make a wonderful memento of a special occasion.

The following conditions will affect your decorated cake:

- Sunlight will fade and alter the colours of icing, so always store in a dark place.
- Humidity can have a disastrous effect on modelling paste and pastillage decorations, causing the icing to become soft and models to droop.
- Heat can melt icing, especially buttercream.

Introducing Colour

When choosing and mixing colours to be used on cakes a basic knowledge of the theory of colour and its application is particularly useful. The subject of colour is a vast and fascinating one, and these basic guidelines will help you to create successful colour schemes for your cakes.

Choosing a colour scheme

There are no right or wrong colour combinations, but the examples on the right are five tried-and-tested schemes that make good starting points from which to experiment:

When you are looking for inspiration for a colour scheme, try looking at the colours that have been used on everyday objects, in magazines, on greetings cards and by artists, as well as those used in other cultures, such as Mexican or African, to discover what combinations appeal to you. You could also try experimenting with paint sample cards, which are available from DIY stores.

The colour wheel

This is a system used by artists. The colours of the spectrum are turned into a circle, which reflects the natural order of the colours. A 12-colour division circle consists of the three primary colours (red, blue and yellow, which are unmixable) three secondary colours (which are mixtures of two primary colours in equal quantities) and six tertiary colours (which are made by mixing primary and secondary colours together; for example, orange mixed with yellow gives yellow-orange).

When you start mixing colours you will find that although in theory the primaries should produce all the other colours, the reality is slightly different; for example, different blues are needed to produce green and violet.

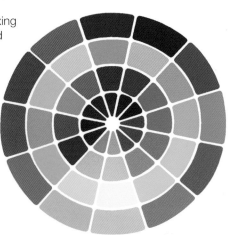

It is helpful to paint a colour wheel yourself, as it will give you the chance to experiment with colour mixing, and will reveal how colours work together.

KEY:
Outer band: hue (pure colour)
Band 2: tints (hue plus white)
Band 3: tones (hue plus grey)
Inner band: shades (hue plus black)

Monochromatic: using tints, tones and shades of just one colour; for example, the different pinks of the roses in Exquisite Bouquet and the swirling gold waves on the Golden Wedding cake (right).

Adjacent: using two, three or four colours lying next to each other on a 12-division colour wheel. The combination produces an easy and pleasing harmony, as the colours are closely related; for example, the design on Art Deco Feathers and the fabrics in Sumptuous Silk (right).

Complementary: using colours that lie opposite or approximately opposite on the wheel. Each pair of colours achieves a balance of cool and warm, as seen with the blue and orange on Birthday Butterfly, red and green on Time for Tea and gold and violet on the Fairytale Castle turrets (right).

Triadic: using three colours equidistantly spaced on the circle, such as the cut-outs used for the nursery decoration on Christening Gift (right).

Polychromatic: using many colours together. This often works effectively using tints, because they are soft colours.

Warm and cold colours – colour temperature

Orange and red are warm colours, whereas blue and green are cold. There are, however, cooler and warmer versions of every colour; for example, red mixed with larger amounts of blue is a cooler colour than a red-orange. Warm colours work especially well on celebration cakes. When placed against a cool colour, a warm colour will appear more intense than if placed against another warm or neutral colour.

1. The warm pinks used on Exquisite Bouquet make it an attractive celebration cake especially suitable for a wedding.

2. The warm-coloured centre of the flower for Birthday Butterfly is prominent against the cold blue of the board.

3. The warm and passionate red heart of Valentine Romance makes a bold statement against the black board.

4. Pastel shades are always appropriate to use on cakes for babies, and the Baby's Blanket cake uses delicate shades of cool colours to good effect.

Colour symbolism

There are both positive and negative symbolic aspects associated with colours, which are familiar to each of us even though we may not be aware of them. This symbolism can be an important consideration when choosing a colour scheme. Below is a range of colours with some of their positive symbolic meanings.

Red	love, passion, excitement, strength
Yellow	sunshine, springtime, youth, cheerfulness, wealth (gold)
Orange	warmth, energy, happiness, vigour
Blue	peace, calm, truth, sea, sky
Green	nature, rest, tranquillity
Violet	luxury, richness, royalty
Black	sophistication, smartness, drama
White	bridal, truth, innocence, delicacy, honesty

Lighting and its effect on colour

When deciding on your colour scheme, bear in mind the lighting that will be used when the cake is displayed, as lighting alters colours considerably. This is especially important for wedding cakes, which are set up in given positions.

Candlelight: many colours disappear, as the light is very weak. If a cake is to be displayed in candlelight use tints, that is, small amounts of colour added to the white paste.

Fluorescent light: this is disastrous with reds, which turn a muddy brown. However, blues are greatly enhanced.

Tungsten lights: this lighting suits reds, oranges and yellow but blues look dull and recessive.

Good daylight: generally the best light in which to display cakes, but daylight's effect on colour depends on which part of the world you live.

Always try to use daylight to select and mix your colours to give the most accurate results.

Colouring sugarpaste and modelling paste

Brightly coloured sugarpaste (rolled fondant) and modelling paste in all kinds of colours are now available commercially. However, if you can't find the exact colour you're searching for, or if only a small amount of a colour is required, it is often best to colour your own paste or adjust the colour of a commercial one. The basic colour-mixing diagram below will give you a quick reference point for mixing paste colours; see the wheel on page 19 for details of the shades you can achieve.

It is easier to colour modelling paste when you are making it before the gum has taken effect.

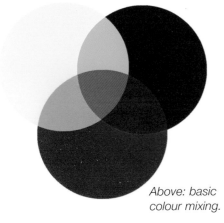

Above: basic colour mixing.

Depending on the amount of paste you wish to colour and the depth of colour required, place a little paste colour, not liquid colour, on the end of a cocktail stick (toothpick) or a larger amount on the end of a palette knife (see picture). Add the colour to the paste and knead in thoroughly, adding more until the desired result is achieved. Be careful with pale colours, as only a little colour is needed. Deep colours, on the other hand, require plenty and will become quite sticky. To overcome this, add a pinch of gum tragacanth and leave for an hour or two; the gum will make the paste firmer and easier to handle. Note: the coloured paste will appear slightly darker when dry.

Painting cakes

You can paint over your cakes, as many fabulous effects can be achieved by painting dried sugarpaste. Painting also helps to brighten the overall appearance of a cake, as even vividly coloured paste will dry with a dull finish. Food colours behave in much the same way as ordinary water-based paints, so you can mix and blend them to produce many different tones and hues.

Allow yourself time to mix your colours as closely as possible to your chosen colour.

To paint sugarpaste, dilute some paste colour in clear spirit, such as gin or vodka, and, using a paintbrush, a damp natural sponge or a stippling brush, apply to the dry sugarpaste. For deep colours, add a little clear spirit to some paste colour. For light colours, or if you want to apply a colour wash, add a little colour to some clear spirit. For details of flood-painting technique see the Stylish Handbag, colouring the board, on page 33.

A stippling brush will give a subtle effect when used to paint sugarpaste.

For flood painting, colour is painted in large strokes, then washed over with clear spirit.

Use a fine paintbrush to add intricate detail to models, such as this butterfly.

The Cakes

Art Deco Feathers

Create this elegant column birthday cake for someone who loves the opulence of feathers and the stylish curves of art deco design. Softly muted colours, influenced by the architect and designer, Charles Rennie Mackintosh (1868–1928), add to its graceful appearance. The cake would also be suitable for an engagement or wedding anniversary. A template has been provided to help you to achieve the design, which is indented on to the sugarpaste and then painted. For a different effect, try the variation – Loops.

Materials

- sugarpaste (rolled fondant): 1.7kg (3¾lb) white
- paste colours: a selection of pinks, blues and purples
- edible dusts: white, silver, snowflake lustre
- clear spirit, such as gin or vodka
- 3 round cakes, each 15cm (6in) in diameter and 7.5cm (3in) deep (see pages 8–11)
- 1 quantity buttercream, or marzipan and apricot glaze (see pages 14–15)
- modelling paste: 25g (1oz) pink, 25g (1oz) light pink, 50g (2oz) white, 25g (1oz) deep pink
- white vegetable fat (shortening)
- a little royal icing
- silver dragées (sugar balls): 50g (2oz) 8–10mm (⁵⁄₁₆–³⁄₈in), a few 6mm (¼in) and 4mm (⅛in)

Equipment

- boards: 25.5cm (10in) round cake drum (board), 2 x 15cm (6in) round hardboard cake boards
- small palette knife
- small natural sponge
- dowels
- 5mm (³⁄₁₆in) spacers, made from strip wood
- smoother
- glass-headed dressmakers' pins
- scriber (optional)
- straightedge or ruler
- cutting wheel
- waxed paper
- circle cutters: 1.5cm (⅝in), 2cm (¾in), 8.5cm (3¼in)
- oval cutters: 2cm (¾in), 2.25cm (⅞in)
- square cutter: 2.5cm (1in)
- ball tool
- paintbrushes
- sugar shaper with medium round and medium ribbon discs
- narrow spacers made from 1.5mm (¹⁄₁₆in) thick card
- posy pick and oasis fix
- feathers: pink, lilac and wine marabou feathers, 2 white ostrich feathers
- wire: pink bullion wire, 1.5mm (¹⁄₁₆in) aluminium wire
- silver-pearl beads: 4 x 8mm (⁵⁄₁₆in), 200 x 4mm (⅛in)
- pink ribbon and non-toxic glue stick
- clear elastic beading cord or white cotton
- jewel glue

Preparation

♥ COVERING THE BOARD ♥

Roll out some of the sugarpaste and use to cover the cake drum. Trim the edges flush with the sides of the board using a small palette knife, taking care to keep the cut vertical. Place to one side to dry.

♥ PAINTING THE BOARD ♥

Mix some of the deep pink paste colour and some white dust colour with clear spirit. Take a damp natural sponge, place it into the colour, then paint the board with the sponge by using short, sweeping curved strokes (**A**). If you have applied too much colour, repeat the above with a clean damp sponge. This will lighten the paint effect. Leave to dry.

♥ MAKING THE TEMPLATE ♥

Enlarge the template, and then, using a pencil, trace the pattern of the cake design on to tracing or greaseproof paper. Cut the paper to the size of the template.

Stage One

♥ PREPARING THE CAKE ♥

For sponge cakes: level the cakes and, if using Madeira, cut away the crusts. Place two cakes individually on the hardboard cake boards, securing the boards in place with buttercream. Dowel the base cake and the middle cake. Spread a thin layer of buttercream over the top of each cake and stack into the required shape. Curve the edge of the top cake with a small carving knife to give it a rounded appearance. Spread a thin layer of buttercream over the cake to stick the sugarpaste.

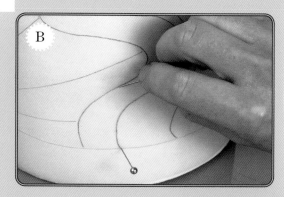

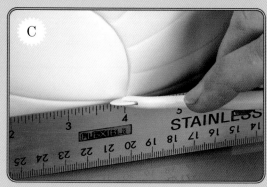

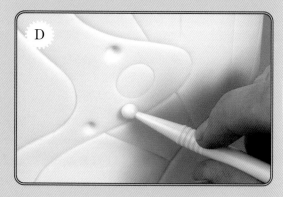

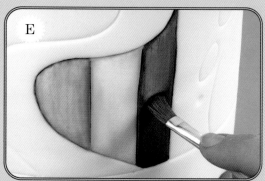

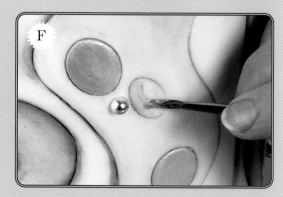

For fruit cakes: invert the cakes. Place two cakes individually on the hardboard cake boards securing the boards in place with boiled apricot glaze. Dowel the base cake and the middle cake and stack. Fill the spaces between the base and the layers with sausages of marzipan to create the column (see page 14) and then cover with marzipan as described for the sugarpaste below. Paint clear spirit over the marzipan to stick the sugarpaste.

> You may wish to freeze the cake at this stage to make rolling it up in sugarpaste easier.

♥ COVERING THE CAKE ♥

1 Knead 1kg (2¼lb) of white sugarpaste, and then roll it out between the 5mm (³⁄₁₆in) spacers. Turn the paste over and cut it into a 30cm (12in) wide x 50cm (20in) long rectangle. Place the cake on its side on to the paste so the base is flush with one long edge. Roll up the cake in the paste and trim as necessary to create a neat, straight join and rub closed using the heat from your hand. (If the join remains visible it can easily be made part of the pattern.)

2 Stand the cake upright on waxed paper and fold the sugarpaste over the top of the cake. Cut away the excess with scissors and, using a smoother, smooth the sides and top of the cake.

♥ ADDING THE PATTERN ♥

1 Working quickly so the sugarpaste does not dry out, place the template around the cake so that the edges meet over the closed join in the sugarpaste. Secure in place with glass-headed pins. Scribe the pattern on to the cake by going over the pencil lines with a scriber or pin (**B**). Remove the pins and template.

2 Place a 3cm (1⅛in) wide straightedge horizontally against the base of the cake and run a cutting wheel along the top edge to indent a band all the way around the base of the cake (**C**).

3 Place a ruler vertically up against the cake where the template joined itself. Run a cutting wheel along the length of the ruler to indent the paste. Repeat for the other vertical lines.

4 Take the cutting wheel and run it over all the curved lines, continuing the lines over the top of the cake.

5 Place the large circle cutter in position on the cake and carefully indent the upper part of the circle by slightly rocking the cutter.

6 Take a ruler and, using a cutting wheel, mark all the rays of the sun. Then, using the small oval and circle cutters, gently press their shapes into the soft paste as indicated on the template. Using the small end of a ball tool, indent holes for the silver balls (**D**).

Stage Two

♥ PAINTING THE CAKE ♥

1 Mix up the suggested paste colours with varying amounts of white dust colour and clear spirit; this makes the colours behave more like acrylics rather than watercolours. Choosing one colour, outline a shape by carefully painting into the indentations around it, then paint the shape itself. With the same colour, repeat for other segments of the design.

2 Once you have applied one colour take a damp brush and start to remove the paste colour from the centre of each painted shape (**E**). This will give dark lines outlining the shape and a graded colour on the segment itself. Repeat for the other colours but leave the ovals and circles and some segments unpainted.

3 Dilute some of the silver dust in clear spirit and paint the ovals and circles (**F**). Mix the snowflake lustre dust with clear spirit and paint over the remaining white shapes. Leave to dry.

Stage Three

♥ THE DECORATIVE BAND ♥

1 Place the painted cake centrally on the cake drum. Soften the light pink modelling paste by kneading in some white vegetable fat to stop the paste becoming sticky and then partially dunk the paste into a small container of boiled water; knead again (the paste should have the consistency of chewing gum). Place the softened paste with the medium round disc into the sugar shaper and squeeze out a length around the base of the cake.

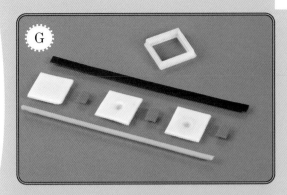

2 Roll out the white and pink modelling pastes between the narrow spacers and cut out 17 white squares, using a cutter, and 17 pink 8mm x 1cm (⁵⁄₁₆ x ⅜in) rectangles (G). Attach these to the cake above the pink trim, as seen on the main photo. Indent the centre of each square with the large end of the ball tool.

3 Soften the deep pink modelling paste as before and place in the sugar shaper with the medium ribbon disc, and squeeze out a length above the white square pattern.

♥ ADDING SILVER BALLS ♥

Place a little oasis fix into the posy pick, and insert the pick into the centre of the cake. Using the royal icing, stick some silver dragées in the indentations in the side of the cake and attach the remaining ones to the top of the cake (H).

♥ THE TOPPER ♥

1 Wire the marabou feathers into groups of three, if you have bought them singularly. Wind the pink bullion wire up the centres of the ostrich feathers adding in a few silver pearl beads as you go – this allows you to adjust the shape at the top of the feather. Cut the aluminium wire into four lengths then bend each into a scroll (I). Stick a large silver bead to the end of each wire. Arrange the wires in the posy pick then add the feathers.

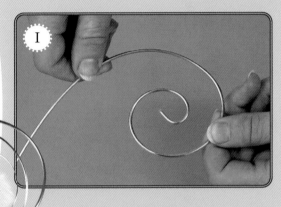

2 Attach the ribbon to the edge of the cake. Thread the 4mm (⅛in) silver-pearl beads on to clear elastic beading cord or white cotton until they fit around the circumference of the cake drum. Tie the ends tightly together and stick in place with jewel glue.

Dress it up

♥ Go to town and add extra tiers for an impressive design to serve a large gathering. You could use a 30cm (12in) cake as the base, topped by a 25.5cm (10in) cake and the Art Deco Feathers design, which is a 15cm (6in) cake.

Dress it down

♥ Omit the painting stage and use white feathers to give a white and silver cake.

Loops

There are all sorts of possible variations that you could make with this cake. I have used straight wires painted pink, loops of aluminium wire and beads, plus loose coils of silver-plated wire to reflect the embossed pattern on the cake itself.

Floral Heart

A heart-shaped cake in pale pink and yellow and decorated with delicate daisies will make the perfect Mother's Day gift. The soft, feminine colours also make it especially attractive as a birthday cake, congratulations cake or welcome-home cake for any woman. This is quite straightforward to make and a template will guide you through creating the wavy join for the two sugarpastes. The flowers are simple to make using a variety of cutters, and are also used as a decoration for the cup cakes.

Materials

- ♥ sugarpaste (rolled fondant): 600g (1lb 5oz) lilac, 350g (12oz) pink, 500g (1lb 2oz) peachy yellow
- ♥ 20cm (8in) Madeira or chocolate heart-shaped cake (see pages 8–11)
- ♥ 1 quantity buttercream
- ♥ white vegetable fat (shortening)

- ♥ modelling paste: 15g (½oz) white, 15g (½oz) deep yellow, 15g (½oz) pink, 25g (1oz) deep pink
- ♥ sugar glue

> If you don't have a heart-shaped tin, bake a 20cm (8in) round cake and carve to shape.

Equipment

- ♥ 28cm (11in) round cake drum (board)
- ♥ small palette knife
- ♥ waxed paper
- ♥ 5mm (³⁄₁₆in) spacers, made from strip wood
- ♥ craft knife
- ♥ smoother
- ♥ narrow spacers made from 1.5mm (¹⁄₁₆in) thick card
- ♥ daisy centre moulds (JEM) (optional)

- ♥ cutters: 1cm (³⁄₈in) micro-daisy cutter (CC), daisy cutters in three sizes (FMM daisy collection nos 3, 4 and 5), 2.5cm (1in) five-petal blossom cutter (FMM), 1.25 cm (½in) miniature blossom plunger cutter (PME)
- ♥ small rolling pin
- ♥ cutting wheel
- ♥ pink sparkly ribbon and non-toxic glue stick

Stage One

♥ COVERING THE BOARD ♥

Roll out the lilac sugarpaste and use to cover the cake drum. Trim the edges flush with the sides of the board using a palette knife, taking care to keep the cut vertical. Place to one side to dry.

♥ CARVING THE CAKE ♥

Level the top of the cake. Using a sharp knife, carefully cut away the cake towards the point to form the tip of the heart, as shown on the carving sketch. Next, carve away the sides of the cake by cutting a gentle curve from the centre of the cake down to all the lower edges (**A**).

The cake can be frozen overnight before being carved if you like.

♥ COVERING THE CAKE ♥

1 Place the cake on waxed paper and spread a thin layer of buttercream over it to stick the sugarpaste.

2 Copy the wave template on to tracing or greaseproof paper and cut carefully along the line. Knead the pink sugarpaste then roll it out between the 5mm (³⁄₁₆in) spacers. Place the wave template on the left-hand side of the paste and, using a sharp craft knife, cut carefully along the outside of the wave (**B**). Pick up the sugarpaste and position the paste on the cake so that the wave runs down the length of the heart slightly to the left-hand side of the cake, referring to the main photo as a guide. Take a smoother and repeatedly run it along the sugarpaste at the base of the cake, gradually pressing down as you do so. When you can see the waxed paper through the paste, trim the excess paste away for a neat finish.

3 Roll out the peachy yellow sugarpaste between the 5mm (³⁄₁₆in) spacers. Cut out the wave as before, but this time placing the template on the right-hand side of the paste. Pick up the sugarpaste and carefully position it on to the cake so that the wave abuts the pink wave on the cake (**C**). Smooth into position and cut away the excess paste as before.

4 Smooth the whole cake by using a smoother to iron out any irregularities in the surface of the icing and then using the base of your hand to smooth and polish all the curves. Allow the sugarpaste to dry.

If your cut around the base isn't that neat you can disguise it with a simple border or a row of hearts or flowers.

Stage Two

♥ DECORATING THE CAKE ♥

1 Carefully lift the cake from its waxed paper and place centrally on the prepared cake board.

2 Thinly roll out some white modelling paste between the narrow spacers then cut out daisies using the micro-daisy cutter. Attach these randomly to the pink half of the cake using sugar glue. Add centres to the daisies by rolling small balls of deep yellow modelling paste and pressing them into a daisy centre mould.

3 For the large daisies, thinly roll out some white modelling paste. Place one of the daisy cutters, cutter side up on your work board or work surface, place the modelling paste over the cutter and roll over it with a small rolling pin (**D**). Run your finger over the edges of the cutter to get a clean cut (**E**), then turn the cutter over and press out the paste. Cut away the petals from one side of the flower and attach them between the remaining petals (**F**). Make one daisy of each size and attach in position on the cake, see main picture for placement guide.

If you don't have a daisy centre mould just roll yellow balls for daisy centres.

4 For the daisy centres, roll a ball of deep yellow modelling paste and press it into a daisy centre mould of an appropriate size. Release the paste from the mould and fold one side over and pinch lightly to shape (**G**). Attach to the centre of a daisy and repeat for the remaining ones.

5 For the small flowers, using the two pink modelling pastes and the blossom cutters, cut a selection of flowers (**H**), and then add small, contrasting balls of paste for their centres.

6 For the leaf, thinly roll out some white modelling paste and cut out a freehand leaf shape using a cutting wheel. Mark a central vein, and then attach to the cake below the flowers (see the main picture for position).

7 To create the bow, thinly roll out the deep pink modelling paste and cut out two 8cm x 8mm (3⅛ x ⁵⁄₁₆in) strips. Fold each strip over to make a loop and attach in position on the cake, see main photo for position. Add a small ball to the centre of the bow.

8 For the stems, take a cutting wheel and carefully indent lines from the flowers to the centre of the bow and out below, so that they look like a tied bunch of flowers (**I**).

9 Using a non-toxic glue stick, attach the ribbon around the side of the board to complete the cake.

Dress it up

♥ Add a suitable message to the board using embossers or letter cutters.

♥ Cover the cake with more ornate or detailed flowers, such as roses (see Sumptuous Silk and Exquisite Bouquet, pages 48 and 94).

Dress it down

♥ If time is short, cover the heart with one colour.

♥ Replace the bunch of flowers with scattered plunger flowers.

♥ Instead of flowers to decorate, make a larger bow.

Cup cakes

Cover the top of each cup cake with a disc of sugarpaste. Make flowers as for the main cake and attach with sugar glue. For the heart, use a heart cutter (FMM) and cut out a pink heart and a yellow heart. Take a craft knife and cut a wave line down the pink heart, place one cut half on top of the yellow heart and cut along the edge of the wave. Remove the top pink half-heart and attach to the cup cake, add the second half of the yellow heart to form a complete shape.

Stylish Handbag

Whether you're making a birthday cake for a fashion-conscious teenager or a groovy granny, this funky handbag is certain to fascinate. It would also be the perfect cake to make for a young woman who is just about to take her first step into the world of work. Simply change the colour and decoration to individualize the design. If you take care over the initial stages of getting the basic shapes correct for the cake and pastillage handle you will find that you can achieve a professional finish. You can also make cup cakes to accompany the cake.

Materials

- 15cm (6in) square Madeira or chocolate cake (see pages 8–11)
- sugarpaste (rolled fondant): 600g (1lb 5oz) ivory, 800g (1¾lb) light cream
- paste colours: yellow, light orange, mid orange
- clear spirit, such as gin or vodka
- 115g (4oz) pastillage
- 1 quantity buttercream
- gum tragacanth
- sugar glue
- white vegetable fat (shortening)
- edible orange dust

It is important with this cake that the preparation is done a few days in advance.

Equipment

- 25.5cm (10in) round cake drum (board)
- small palette knife
- paintbrushes
- thin card
- sticky tape
- narrow spacers made from 1.5mm (⅟₁₆in) thick card
- waxed paper
- 5mm (³⁄₁₆in) spacers, made from strip wood
- straightedge, such as a ruler
- smoother
- set square
- craft knife
- cutting wheel
- sugar shaper with the medium round disc (optional)
- large daisy cutter (no. 2 from the FMM daisy collection)
- CelPad (optional)
- ball tool
- daisy centre moulds (JEM) (optional)
- orange ribbon and non-toxic glue stick

Preparation

♥ PREPARING THE CAKE FOR FREEZING ♥
Level the cake, and if using Madeira, remove the crusts. Freeze overnight.

♥ COVERING AND DECORATING THE BOARD ♥
Roll out the ivory sugarpaste, using icing (confectioners') sugar or white fat to prevent sticking. Use to cover the cake drum. Trim the edges flush with the sides of the board using a small palette knife, taking care to keep the cut vertical.

♥ COLOURING THE BOARD ♥
(FLOOD PAINTING)

1 Slightly dilute each of the yellow and orange paste colours separately with clear spirit. Take a large paintbrush and roughly paint each colour in sections over the board leaving some areas white (**A**).

2 Carefully pour clear spirit or cooled boiled water over the partially painted surface (**B**), then use a paintbrush to encourage the liquid to cover the board entirely (**C**). (You may wish to try this effect on a spare piece of sugarpaste first.) The liquid will melt the surface of the paste so that the colours merge; be patient, as this takes a few minutes. Leave undisturbed on a level surface to dry thoroughly.

♥ PASTILLAGE HANDLE ♥

1 Transfer the handle template on to a piece of paper, drawing around a 13cm (5in) circle to achieve a smooth curve. Cut a strip of thin card about 3cm (1⅛in) wide. Secure the card strip around the edge of the template using tape, and make two folds at the corners (see picture **D**).

2 Using the narrow spacers, roll out a long length of pastillage, and then cut it into a 1.75cm (⅝in) wide strip.

3 Place the strip around the former (**D**). Leave to dry. An airing cupboard is an excellent place to dry pastillage.

> An excellent tool for cutting strips is a multi-ribbon cutter (FMM).

Stage One

♥ CARVING THE CAKE ♥

Referring to the carving sketch for guidance, cut away two 4cm (1½in) deep tapered triangles from either side of the square cake. Place the cake on its uncut edge then carefully cut a thin wedge away from the front and back of the bag so that the top is slightly narrower than the base. Next, curve all the cut edges and then cut away a small wedge all the way around the base of the bag to give a rounded appearance (see picture **E**).

♥ COVERING THE CAKE ♥

1 Place the cake on waxed paper and spread a thin layer of buttercream over it to stick the sugarpaste (**E**). Knead the light cream sugarpaste and roll out half between the 5mm (³⁄₁₆in) spacers. Cut one edge straight, pick up the paste and place on the front of the cake with the cut edge at the base of the cake. Smooth the paste around the sides of the cake and over the top.

2 Take the set square and place it centrally up against one side of the cake. Cut vertically along the edge of the set square with a palette knife (**F**), and remove the excess sugarpaste (**G**). Repeat for the other side, and then cut across the top.

3 Roll out the second half of the sugarpaste. Cut one edge straight and position on the cake. Cut away the excess paste as before so that the paste on the sides abuts. Smooth the front and sides of the cake with a smoother, then press a straightedge along the joins on the sides to neaten. Allow the sugarpaste to dry.

♥ MAKING MODELLING PASTE ♥

1 Take 100g (3½oz) of the cream sugarpaste trimmings and knead in 2.5ml (½tsp) of gum tragacanth to make modelling paste. Colour 25g (1oz) orange and 15g (½oz) yellow.

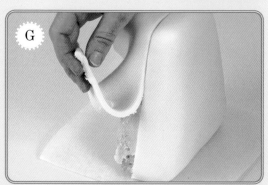

2 Leave the paste to mature, ideally overnight.

> If pushed for time use CMC instead of gum tragacanth, as it reacts much quicker.

Stage Two

♥ THE HANDLE ♥

1 Lift the cake from its waxed paper, and place centrally on the prepared board.

2 Carefully lift the completely dried handle from its card former and insert into the top of the cake. Cover the pastillage handle with sugar glue. Roll out the cream modelling paste between narrow spacers and cut out a 26 x 4.5cm (10¼ x 1¾in) strip.

3 Carefully place the strip on top of the handle, easing the paste over the edges and under to meet in the middle. Cut the strip to size with a craft knife where the handle meets the bag on either side.

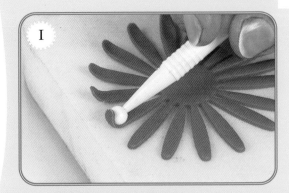

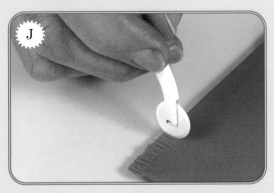

♥ THE OPENING FLAP ♥

1 Transfer the flap template to tracing or greaseproof paper and adjust it to fit your cake, if necessary.

2 Roll out the cream modelling paste between the narrow spacers, place the template on the paste and cut out with a cutting wheel. Attach the flap to the cake with sugar glue, ensuring that the paste is positioned centrally between the handle.

3 Soften some cream modelling paste. Do this by firstly kneading in some white vegetable fat to stop the paste becoming sticky and then partially dunk the paste into a small container of boiled water before kneading again (the paste should have the consistency of chewing gum). Place the softened paste with the medium round disc into the sugar shaper and squeeze out two short lengths. Place the lengths around the handle joins, cutting them flush with the edges of the opening flap using a craft knife. (Alternatively roll a thin sausage of modelling paste by hand and attach as above.)

♥ THE FLOWER ♥

1 Roll out the orange modelling paste between the narrow spacers. Place the large daisy cutter, cutter side up, on your work board or work surface, place the modelling paste over the cutter and roll over it with a small rolling pin. Run your finger over the edges of the cutter to obtain a clean cut (**H**), and then turn the cutter over and carefully press out the paste.

2 Place the modelling-paste daisy on a CelPad, or the palm of your hand, and run the small end of a ball tool from the tip of a petal towards the centre (**I**) to curl the ends.

3 Cut out a second daisy, curl the ends of the petals and place on top of the first.

4 Thinly roll out a strip of orange paste and cut into the edge repeatedly with a cutting wheel (**J**). Place the strip around the edge of the flower centre.

5 Roll a ball of yellow modelling paste and press it into the daisy centre mould before attaching it to the flower. Add a narrower orange strip around the yellow centre, and then, using a paintbrush, dust the very centre of the flower with orange dust.

♥ FINISHING TOUCHES ♥

Attach the flower to the cake with sugar glue then, using a non-toxic glue stick, attach the ribbon around the sides of the board to complete the cake.

Dress it up

♥ For the fashion-conscious girl who's having a big party, why not place the bag on a larger vanity-case cake, model all her favourite accessories and scatter these around the cakes – it's sure to be a big hit!

Dress it down

♥ If you are short of time, create the cake lying on its back. Carve the cake as above, place on its back on waxed paper then cover with sugarpaste. Once dry, transfer to a prepared board. Make the flap and flower as above then model a handle from modelling paste.

♥ Simplify the handle by making a simple shoulder strap instead.

Cup cakes

Cover the top of each cup cake with a disc of sugarpaste. Make flowers as for the main cake or make a variety of different ones in the same colours, as shown below, and attach with sugar glue.

Christening Gift

Delicate pink hearts and lilac flowers burst from the top of this delightfully decorated baby girl's christening cake. The cake is covered with sugarpaste and the frilled 'paper' top is created using modelling paste. The cake could easily be adapted to be suitable for a baby boy's christening by using blue for the bow and nursery cut-outs. Wired decorations make a stunning 'topper' for all kinds of cakes, and this cake could easily be transformed into a birthday or congratulations cake for a child, teenager or adult – simply change the colours for the box and decorations, and use different cut-outs for the motifs. Matching cup cakes are included.

Equipment

- ♥ waxed paper
- ♥ 5mm (³⁄₁₆in) spacers, made from strip wood
- ♥ smoother
- ♥ posy pick
- ♥ 25.5cm (10in) square cake drum (board)
- ♥ small palette knife
- ♥ narrow spacers made from 1.5mm (¹⁄₁₆in) thick card
- ♥ craft knife
- ♥ paintbrush
- ♥ thin card
- ♥ small pieces of foam

- ♥ cutters: nursery cutters (PC Make a Cradle set and nursery set; also toy tappits by FMM), leaf heart cutters (T), 2.5cm (1in) five-petal blossom cutter (FMM), small teardrop cutter, set of miniature blossom plunger cutters (PME)
- ♥ silver 26 gauge straight floristry wires
- ♥ plastic embossing strip or textured rolling pin
- ♥ a little oasis fix
- ♥ pink ribbons and non-toxic glue stick

Materials

- ♥ 2 x 15cm (6in) square Madeira or chocolate cakes (see pages 8–11)
- ♥ 1 quantity buttercream
- ♥ sugarpaste (rolled fondant): 1kg (2¼lb) white, 800g (1¾lb) pale pink

- ♥ white vegetable fat (shortening)
- ♥ modelling paste: 125g (4½oz) pink, 25g (1oz) mint green, 25g (1oz) golden brown, 25g (1oz) lilac, 225g (8oz) white
- ♥ sugar glue

Stage One

♥ CARVING THE CAKE ♥

Level the cakes and cut away the crusts. Spread a thin layer of buttercream over the top of one cake and stack the other on top. Take a small carving knife and curve all the edges, then place on waxed paper.

♥ COVERING THE CAKE ♥

1 Spread a thin layer of buttercream over the cake to stick the sugarpaste. Roll out the white sugarpaste, preferably between 5mm (³⁄₁₆in) spacers, and cut into a 58cm (22¾in) long 23cm (9in) wide strip. Carefully roll up the paste, like a bandage, and position it against the side of the cake. Next, unroll the paste around the cake and rub the join closed.

2 Ease the sugarpaste over the top edge of the cake, encouraging the paste to form in folds. Tuck the sugarpaste under the base of the cake, and then use a smoother to create a flat finish to the sides of the cake. Polish all the curved edges of the cube with the palm of your hand, and then, using a finger, rub the folds of sugarpaste on the top of the cake to soften and adjust their shape (**A**). Mark the centre of the top of the cake and vertically insert a posy pick, leaving it standing 1cm (³⁄₈in) proud of the top (**B**). Leave to dry.

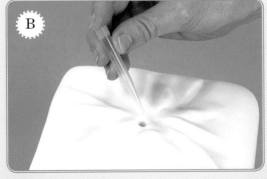

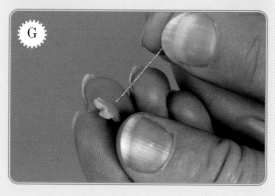

♥ COVERING THE BOARD ♥

Roll out the pink sugarpaste and use to cover the cake drum. Trim the edges flush with the sides of the board using a small palette knife, taking care to keep the cut vertical.

Stage Two

♥ DECORATING THE CAKE ♥

1 Carefully lift the cake from its waxed paper and place centrally on the prepared cake board.

2 Roll out some of the pink modelling paste between the narrow spacers and cut out eight pink rabbits with the FMM toy tappit cutter (**C**) and hearts with the leaf heart cutter. Using sugar glue, attach one or two of each design per side. Cut out rocking horses and teddies from thinly rolled mint and golden-brown modelling pastes respectively. Attach randomly to the cake.

3 To make the stacks of alphabet bricks, cut out sets of bricks from the pink, lilac and golden-brown modelling pastes. Then separate the bricks with a craft knife before attaching them to the cake using one brick of each colour in each group (**D**).

4 Make small lilac flowers using the blossom cutters, and attach to the cake. Add a centre to each flower by rolling and attaching a small ball of golden paste. Cut leaves using the small teardrop cutter, and attach to the cake using a paintbrush (**E**).

♥ THE FRILL ♥

1 Cut out a 25.5cm (10in) diameter circle from thin card and remove a 4cm (1½in) circle from its centre. Cut away a quarter of the circle, and then roll the remainder into a cone and stick the edges together. Balance the cone on top of the present (see picture **F**).

2 Roll out the white modelling paste into a strip between the narrow spacers. Cut the strip to a width of 9cm (3½in) and length of 60cm (24in). Gather up one long edge, paint it with sugar glue and place it around the protruding posy pick inside the card cone. Arrange the paste to form folds using small pieces of foam to support them (**F**). Place to one side to dry thoroughly.

♥ THE TOPPER ♥

1 Thinly roll out some white modelling paste between the narrow spacers and cut out six 2.5cm (1in) blossoms. Add a golden centre to each. Dip six silver wires into the sugar glue and insert one into the side of each flower. Place on foam to dry.

2 Cut out a selection of lilac flowers using the blossom plunger, adding golden centres as before. Insert wires into the sides of the larger flowers and into the backs of the smaller ones (**G**).

3 Make eight pink hearts from modelling paste and insert the wires up through the point of the hearts. Place on foam to dry.

Stage Three

♥ THE BOW ♥

1 Remove the card cone from the top of the cake.

2 Thinly roll out some pink modelling paste and emboss it with a plastic embossing strip (**H**) or use a textured rolling pin. Cut the paste into four 3cm (1½in) wide strips.

> A multi-ribbon cutter is an excellent tool for cutting strips.

3 For the ribbon tails, cut across one strip at an angle, and then cut to a length of 8cm (3¼in). Gather the top of each tail. Repeat for the second tail, cutting a mirror image.

4 For the loops, cut a strip to a length of 20cm (8in). Mark the centre and bring the ends in to make the loops. Slightly squeeze the centre together (**I**). Finish off the loops by wrapping a 5cm (2in) strip around their centre. Attach a further strip around the base of the paste cone and then attach the tails and the loops in place.

♥ ARRANGING THE TOPPER ♥

1 Place a small amount of oasis fix into the posy pick to help secure the wires for the topper.

2 Take a wired white flower and gently curve the wire by wrapping it around a cylinder shape, such as a bottle or drinks can (**J**). Cut the wire to an appropriate length for your cake and insert into the posy pick so that the flower rests at about the same height as the top of the cake. Repeat for the other white flowers.

3 Create the basic shape of the topper by adding the pink hearts to the centre to define the height, cut the wire of each heart so that it is at a different height.

4 Fill in the space between the hearts and white flowers with the remaining lilac flowers, bending the wires as before and making sure that they are evenly spaced.

♥ FINISHING TOUCHES ♥

Using a non-toxic glue stick, attach the ribbons around the sides of the board to complete the cake.

Dress it up

♥ Add the baby's name to the cake using letter cutters.

♥ For a larger celebration, make the cake larger to serve more people or make additional smaller present cakes and arrange them around the main present. Or you could make a larger present and stack the cube present on top.

Dress it down

♥ Omit the posy pick and wires.

♥ Have fewer decorations and a plain bow.

♥ Use a few bought dainty fabric flowers in the posy pick instead of the wires.

♥ Omit the frill and have a large fabric bow on top instead.

Cup cakes

Cover the top of each cup cake with a disc of pink sugarpaste, and then add a smaller circle of white modelling paste. Decorate each cake using the cutters and modelling pastes used for the main cake.

Time for Tea

Needing a cake for an afternoon party, or for mum or a favourite aunt who just loves tea? Look no further – here is a novelty cake that will fit the bill perfectly. A ball cake is covered with sugarpaste and the handle and spout are formed from pastillage covered with modelling paste. A template will help you to create the shapes. The design is quite simple, but you can change the colours and decoration to suit the recipient; there are many other embossers that you could use. Continue the design on to the accompanying cup cakes.

Materials

- ♥ sugarpaste (rolled fondant): 500g (1lb 2oz) red, 800g (1¾lb) ivory
- ♥ 25g (1oz) pastillage
- ♥ white vegetable fat (shortening)
- ♥ ½ quantity buttercream, or marzipan and apricot glaze (see pages 14–15)
- ♥ 13cm (5in) ball cake (see pages 8–11)
- ♥ gum tragacanth
- ♥ paste colours: green, black
- ♥ sugar glue

Equipment

- ♥ 28 x 23cm (11 x 9in) oval cake drum (board)
- ♥ small palette knife
- ♥ sugar shaper with small round, medium round, large round and medium ribbon discs
- ♥ waxed paper
- ♥ 5mm (³⁄₁₆in) spacers
- ♥ smoother
- ♥ poppy embosser/cutter (PC)
- ♥ dowel
- ♥ narrow spacers made from 1.5mm (¹⁄₁₆in) thick card
- ♥ craft knife
- ♥ foam for support
- ♥ 4mm (⅛in) spacers, made from strip wood
- ♥ circle cutters: 7cm (2¾in), 2.5cm (1in)
- ♥ cutting wheel
- ♥ red ribbon and non-toxic glue stick

Preparation

♥ COVERING THE BOARD ♥

Roll out the red sugarpaste and use to cover the cake drum. Trim the edges flush with the sides of the board using a small palette knife, taking care to keep the cut vertical.

♥ PASTILLAGE PIECES ♥

1 Transfer the teapot template on to a piece of paper, drawing around a 13cm (5in) circle to achieve a smooth curve.

2 Knead the pastillage and add a small amount of white fat to prevent the paste becoming sticky. Partially dunk the pastillage into a small container of cooled boiled water and knead until the paste is soft and smooth. Roll the pastillage into a sausage and place inside the sugar shaper with the large round disc. Squeeze out a length and place over the line inside the spout on the template (**A**) and cut to size.

3 Next, squeeze out a length over the handle of the template making a small indentation where it crosses the outside of the teapot. Leave to dry thoroughly; this could take a few days so allow yourself time.

An airing cupboard is an excellent place to dry pastillage

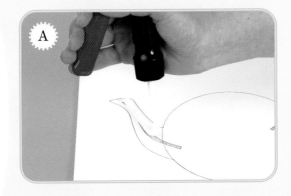

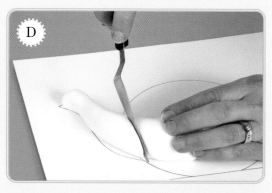

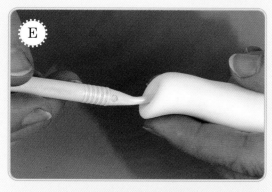

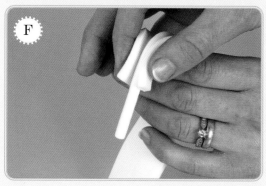

Stage One

♥ COVERING THE CAKE ♥

1 Place the cake on waxed paper, and spread a thin layer of buttercream over it to stick the sugarpaste (if using a fruit cake, cover with apricot glaze and marzipan). Knead the ivory sugarpaste to warm it, and then roll out between the 5mm (³⁄₁₆in) spacers. Pick up the paste and carefully place it over the cake so that the paste meets the base of one side of the ball and goes over the top to the base on the other side. Encourage the excess paste into two pleats on opposite sides of the ball, where the spout and handle will be situated.

2 Take a sharp pair of scissors and cut away the pleats so that the sugarpaste is flush with the cake. Using a combination of a smoother and the palm of your hand, smooth the sugarpaste to blend the joins. As long as you keep working the paste it will remain pliable. The joins should completely disappear, but don't worry if any remain, as the spout and handle should cover them.

3 Take the poppy cutter and carefully emboss poppies on either side of the cake. As the cake is round and the cutter is flat, do this by placing the cutter centrally in position (**B**), then carefully rocking it up and down and from side to side. Don't worry if the embossing isn't perfect: it is only there as a guide when placing on the poppy pieces. Allow the sugarpaste to dry.

♥ MAKING MODELLING PASTE ♥

Add a pinch of gum tragacanth to 15g (½oz) red sugarpaste. Add 5ml (1 tsp) of gum to 225g (8oz) of ivory sugarpaste, and then colour 15g (½oz) green and 25g (1oz) black using paste colour. Leave to mature overnight.

Stage Two

♥ PREPARING THE CAKE ♥

1 Carefully lift the cake from its waxed paper and place centrally on the prepared board.

2 Using the template to indicate the position and angle, insert a dowel into the cake where the spout is to go, then remove. Repeat for the handle, inserting the dowel on the opposite side of the cake, then remove.

♥ POPPY ♥

Roll out all the modelling pastes, except for the ivory, between the narrow spacers. Emboss the poppy using the poppy cutter on to the red paste, the leaves and poppy centre on to the green, and base of petals on to the black. Use a craft knife held vertically to cut along the embossed lines of the shapes (**C**). Next, attach the modelling paste pieces to their positions on the cake using sugar glue. Repeat for the second poppy.

♥ SPOUT ♥

Roll out a large, tapered sausage of ivory modelling paste to fit the spout template, make a cut through the paste along the line of the main cake section (**D**). Push a dowel up through the spout and remove, then cover the prepared pastillage with glue and insert into the prepared hole in the spout. Shape the tip of the spout, and then take a Dresden tool and indent the pouring hole (**E**). Insert the spout into the prepared hole in the cake, attaching it with sugar glue. Support it in place with foam if necessary.

If the weather is particularly damp you can give the spout extra support by inserting 2.5cm (1in) of a 7.5cm (3in) dowel at an angle into the modelling paste just underneath the pastillage. Push the remainder of the dowel into the cake.

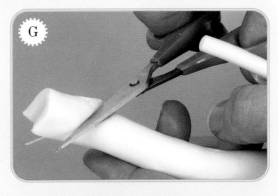

♥ HANDLE ♥

Roll out the remaining ivory modelling paste between the 4mm (⅛in) spacers and cut out a 3.25cm (1¼in) wide 16cm (6¼in) long strip. Paint glue over the prepared pastillage handle leaving the section to be inserted into the cake unpainted. Place the strip under the handle and enclose the pastillage with the modelling paste (**F**). Smooth the join closed then cut off the excess at the base of the handle with scissors (**G**). Insert the top of the handle into the prepared hole in the cake, checking that it is in line with the spout, and leave to dry.

> Look at an actual teapot for a guide to spout and handle shape.

♥ LID ♥

Roll out the red and black modelling pastes between the narrow spacers. Cut out a 7cm (2¾in) red circle and 2.5cm (1in) black circle. Glue the black on top of the red and place on top of the teapot for a lid. Top this with a ball rolled from the remaining green modelling paste.

Stage Three

♥ FINISHING TOUCHES ♥

1 Soften some ivory modelling paste by adding white fat to stop it becoming sticky, and boiled water to soften it. Place this softened paste into a sugar shaper with the medium ribbon disc and squeeze out a length to cover the join line on the outside of the handle. Attach in place.

2 Remove the ribbon disc and replace it with the small round disc and squeeze out paste to neaten the joins between the spout and the cake, and the handle and the cake (**H**).

3 Soften some black modelling paste, and insert into the sugar shaper with the medium round disc. Squeeze out a sausage of paste to go around the base of the teapot. Attach in place.

> You can use a sharp craft knife to adjust the shape of the lip of the spout, if required.

4 Using a non-toxic glue stick attach the ribbon around the side of the cake board to complete the cake.

Cup cakes

Cover the top of each cup cake with a disc of ivory sugarpaste. Make the poppies as for the main cake and position one on to the cup cake slightly off-centre. Trim the edge to fit. Make the remaining cakes so that each is slightly different, to achieve a striking effect.

Dress it up

♥ Make the board into a tray by adding a lip and handles.

♥ Use a larger board and add a moulded sugar bowl or a cup and saucer and, perhaps, a plate of biscuits. Just let your imagination go.

Dress it down

♥ Choose a bright colour for the teapot and make it all in the same colour but decorate it all over with simple cut-out flowers.

♥ Choose one colour for the teapot and then other bright and contrasting colours for the lid, handle and spout – perhaps go for bold pinks, violets and blues.

Valentine Romance

Create this luxurious heart-shaped cake for Valentine's Day or another romantic occasion, such as an engagement celebration. Red sugarpaste covers the cake and it is decorated with modelling-paste swirls. A stunning effect is achieved by making a golden pastillage arrow, which pierces the heart. This is a fairly straightforward cake to make, but take care when you form the delicate arrow and position it through the cake. Heart cup cakes continue the theme.

Materials

- 100g (3½oz) pastillage
- golden-brown paste colour
- edible gold dust
- white vegetable fat (shortening)
- sugar glue
- sugarpaste (rolled fondant): 600g (1lb 5oz) black, 750g (1lb 10oz) red
- icing (confectioners') sugar
- 20cm (8in) Madeira or chocolate heart-shaped cake (see pages 8–11)
- 1 quantity buttercream
- confectioners' glaze
- 50g (2oz) modelling paste
- gold dragées (sugar balls)

Dragées are useful for the celebration cake-decorator's store cupboard.

Equipment

- narrow spacers made from 1.5mm (⅟₁₆in) thick card
- cutting wheel
- foam for drying
- craft knife
- sugar shaper with large round and small round discs
- small scissors
- smoother
- paintbrushes
- 30cm (12in) round cake drum (board)
- small palette knife
- waxed paper
- large stippling brush
- glass-headed dressmakers' pins
- scriber (optional)
- 2 dowels
- red and narrow gold ribbons and non-toxic glue stick

Preparation

♥ THE ARROW ♥

1 Colour the pastillage a similar colour to the edible gold dust by using the golden-brown paste colour. Smear your work board with white vegetable fat and roll out a small amount of pastillage between the narrow spacers. Place the arrowhead template on top of the pastillage then carefully cut around it with a cutting wheel (**A**). Lift the cut shape from your work board and place it on foam to dry thoroughly.

2 Roll out some more pastillage. Using the flight template, cut out three flights. Mark the flight feathers on each side of each piece by using a craft knife. Place on foam to dry.

3 To make the shaft for the base of the arrow, soften the remaining pastillage by adding some white fat to stop it sticking and boiled water to soften it. Place the pastillage inside the sugar shaper with the large round disc, and squeeze out a length (**B**). Cut the length to 15cm (6in) with a small pair of scissors. Place on foam and straighten using a smoother. Leave to dry thoroughly.

Pastillage crusts over very quickly so work as speedily as you can.

A

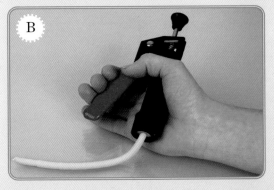

B

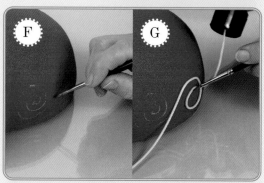

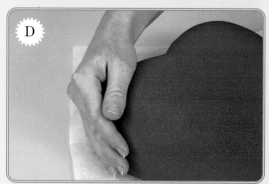

4 Once the arrowhead is dry, squeeze a second piece of pastillage from the sugar shaper. Roll one end to a point and then make a cut lengthways through the point with a small pair of scissors. Paint a line of sugar glue down the centre of each side of the arrowhead and insert the head between the cut ends of the shaft (**C**). Cut the shaft to an overall length of 10cm (4in) and place on foam to dry.

5 Once the flights are dry, carefully attach one to the end of the shaft for the base of the arrow. Use sugar glue, and support the flight in position while the glue dries. Once dry, attach the second flight. When that has dried, position the third flight.

Stage One

♥ COVERING THE BOARD ♥

Roll out the black sugarpaste, using icing sugar or white fat to prevent sticking, and use to cover the board. Trim the edges flush with the sides of the board, taking care to keep the cut vertical. Place to one side to dry.

♥ CARVING THE CAKE ♥

Level the top of the cake and trim the crust from the base. Using a sharp knife, carefully cut away the cake towards the point to form the tip of the heart, as illustrated on page 99. Next, carve away the sides of the cake by cutting a gentle curve from the centre of the cake down to all the lower edges.

♥ COVERING THE CAKE ♥

Place the cake on waxed paper and spread a thin layer of buttercream over it to stick the sugarpaste. Knead the red sugarpaste, and then roll it out and use to cover the cake. Carefully trim the excess paste away from the base of the cake. Smooth the cake by firstly using a smoother to iron out any irregular areas in the surface of the icing and then using the base of your hand to smooth and polish all the curves (**D**). Allow the sugarpaste to dry.

Stage Two

♥ GLAZING THE CAKE BOARD ♥

Pour some confectioners' glaze on to a small plate or similar. Take the stippling brush, dip it into the glaze and then stipple over the entire surface of the covered board. Don't worry that small air bubbles appear in the wet glaze, they disappear as the glaze dries (**E**).

Note: glazing the board is optional, but it does prevent the cake making the black sugarpaste underneath it soft and therefore rather messy to eat. If you don't glaze the board, you can cut a heart-shaped piece of waxed paper slightly smaller than the cake itself and place it under the cake to act as a barrier; this is especially important if the cake you are using is very moist.

Stippling the glaze rather than painting it prevents streaks appearing when it dries.

♥ DECORATING THE CAKE ♥

1 Carefully lift the cake from its waxed paper and place centrally on the glazed board. Dip a fine paintbrush into the sugar glue. Starting at the top of the heart, paint a freehand swirl on to the side of the cake (**F**).

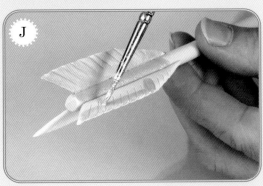

2 Colour the modelling paste a similar colour to the gold dust using the golden-brown paste colour. Soften it by adding a little white vegetable fat, to stop it sticking, and boiled water to soften it. Place the softened paste in the sugar shaper with the small round disc, and squeeze out a length.

> *The softened modelling paste should be the consistency of chewing gum – soft and stretchy.*

3 Place the length over the painted glue swirl and adjust its shape with a finger and/or a paintbrush (**G**). Cut the paste at either end of the swirl with the tip of a small palette knife. Add more swirls, gradually reducing their height towards the tip of the heart (see main picture).

4 Take the hearts template and place on top of the cake. Once you are happy with its position, secure in place with glass-headed pins. Take a scriber or pin and scribe over the lines of the template and around the edges (**H**). Make the hearts in the same way as the scrolls on the side of the cake.

5 To attach the small gold dragées, take a paintbrush and dip it in the sugar glue. Paint dots of glue in spaces between the scrolls and around the top hearts. Place a gold dragée over a glue dot and press it fractionally into the surface of the sugarpaste to secure. Repeat with the other dragées.

♥ **GILDING** ♥

Mix some of the gold dust with some confectioners' glaze and, taking a fine paintbrush, paint over each of the swirls (**I**). Then take a broader brush and paint over both sections of the arrow (**J**).

♥ **INSERTING THE ARROW** ♥

Decide on the entry and exit points of the arrow, and then make holes in the cake with a dowel before inserting the arrow sections, ensuring that they look in line.

> *Be very careful with the arrow sections, as pastillage is very brittle.*

♥ **ADDING RIBBONS** ♥

Using a non-toxic glue stick, attach the ribbons around the sides of the board to complete the cake.

Cup cakes

Cover the top of each cup cake with a disc of red sugarpaste. Take a heart cutter of an appropriate size and indent the front heart. Holding the cutter at a slight angle, indent the second heart behind the first, taking care not to indent lines within the first. Add the gold trims as for the main cake.

Dress it up
♥ Place the couple's initials on either side of the hearts on top of the cake.

Dress it down
♥ Omit the golden pastillage arrow, leaving just the heart-shaped cake.

Sumptuous Silk

The height and form of column cakes gives them impact, and this exquisite fabric-effect cake has curved jewellery wires to increase its elegance. It would be appropriate for a number of occasions, such as a small wedding, engagement party or birthday. The modelling-paste 'fabric' is cut freehand, giving you plenty of scope to be creative. Continue the fabric effect on dainty cup cakes.

Materials

- ♥ 2 x 13cm (5in) cakes, 7.5cm (3in) deep (see pages 8–11)
- ♥ 1 quantity buttercream or marzipan and apricot glaze (see pages 14–15)
- ♥ 1.3kg (3lb) white sugarpaste
- ♥ 65g (2¼oz) deep pink flowerpaste (petal/gum paste), or use modelling paste
- ♥ modelling paste: 100g (3½oz) light pink, 150g (5oz) violet, 100g (3½oz) mid pink, 150g (5oz) white, 100g (3½oz) lilac, 150g (5oz) deep pink
- ♥ white vegetable fat (shortening)
- ♥ sugar glue
- ♥ 8–10mm (⁵⁄₁₆–⅜in) silver dragées (sugar balls)

Equipment

- ♥ 5mm (³⁄₁₆in) spacers, made from strip wood
- ♥ waxed paper
- ♥ smoother
- ♥ 25.5cm (10in) round cake drum (board)
- ♥ small palette knife
- ♥ sugar shaper with medium round and large rope discs (optional)
- ♥ narrow spacers made from 1.5mm (¹⁄₁₆in) thick card
- ♥ cutting wheel
- ♥ posy pick and oasis fix
- ♥ 0.6mm silver jewellery wire (LC)
- ♥ pliers
- ♥ ribbon and non-toxic glue stick
- ♥ diamanté trim and jewel glue
- ♥ glass-headed dressmakers' pins

Stage One

♥ COVERING THE CAKE ♥

Level the cakes and, if using Madeira, cut away the crusts.

♥ SPONGE CAKES ♥

1 Spread a thin layer of buttercream over the top of one cake and stack the other on top. Take a small carving knife and curve the edge of the top cake to give it a more rounded appearance.

2 Spread a thin layer of buttercream over the cake to stick the sugarpaste.

You may find it easier to freeze the cake partially at this stage.

♥ FRUIT CAKES ♥

1 Invert the cakes and stack using boiled apricot glaze to stick them. Fill the spaces between the base and the layers with sausages of marzipan to create the column (see page 14) and then cover with marzipan as described below.

2 Knead 800g (1¾lb) of white sugarpaste and then roll it out between the 5mm (³⁄₁₆in) spacers.

3 Turn the paste over and cut it into a 24–26cm (9½–10¼in) wide x 40.5cm (16in) long rectangle. Place the cake on to the paste so the base is flush with one long edge. Roll up the cake in the paste (**A**) and trim as necessary to create a neat join – the join will be covered at a later stage.

4 Stand the cake upright on waxed paper and fold the sugarpaste over the top of the cake. Cut away the excess with scissors (**B**) but do not worry about creating a flat top. Using a smoother, smooth the sides of the cake then place to one side to dry.

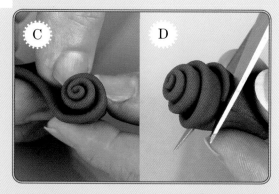

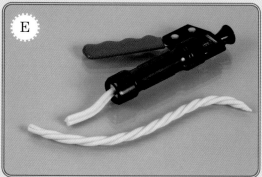

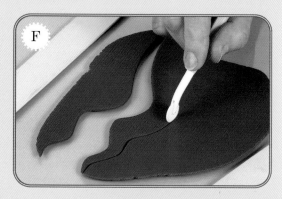

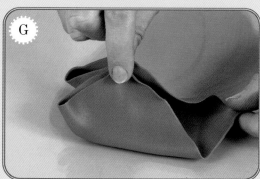

♥ **COVERING THE BOARD** ♥

Roll out some of the sugarpaste and use it to cover the cake drum. Trim the edges flush with the sides of the board using a small palette knife, taking care to keep the cut vertical. Place to one side to dry.

Stage Two

♥ **FABRIC ROSES** ♥

1 Thinly roll out the deep pink flowerpaste.

2 Fold over a section of paste and cut the fold to a width of 1.5cm (⅝in) and length of 13cm (5in). Starting at one end of the folded paste, roll up the paste to form a spiral, pressing the cut edge together and gathering it slightly as you roll to create fullness and space in the flower (**C**). Neaten the back of the rose by cutting off the excess paste with scissors (**D**). Make at least six of these, plus extras for cup cakes if you are making these too.

> It is often easier to roll the flowerpaste into a sausage the correct length before rolling it flat with a rolling pin.

3 Make the large rose as above, but use a folded strip and cut to a width of 7cm (2¾in) and length of 35.5cm (14in).

♥ **DECORATION AROUND THE BASE** ♥

1 Attach the cake to the centre of the prepared cake drum. Soften some light pink modelling paste. Do this by kneading in some white vegetable fat to stop the paste becoming sticky, and then partially dunk the paste into a small container of boiled water before kneading again (the paste should have the consistency of chewing gum). Place the softened paste with the medium round disc into the sugar shaper and squeeze out a length around the base of the cake. Alternatively, roll a sausage of paste by hand.

2 Take four of the fabric roses and, using sugar glue, attach them to the pink trim at the front of the cake at about 3cm (1⅛in) intervals. Place a dragée between each rose.

♥ **ADDING FABRIC** ♥

LAYER 1

1 Roll out the violet modelling paste between the narrow spacers cut to an approximate size of 12 x 25cm (4¾ x 9⅞in). Drape the paste over the top of the cake and down the right-hand side of the roses. Take a cutting wheel and cut the edge of the drape into smooth curves as it rests on the board.

2 Next, roll out the mid pink modelling paste, create three pleats in the paste and place it so that the lower edge hangs at an angle above the roses on the base.

> You don't need to follow my instructions word for word as shapes are cut freehand – go with what feels right to you.

3 Add a white drape to the left of the pleated pink, creating it as the violet one above. Then add a thinner lilac drape to abut the violet. Add movement to one edge by encouraging the paste away from the side of the cake.

LAYER 2

1 Change the disc in the sugar shaper to the large rope, squeeze out a length, twist it (**E**) and drape it over the cake so that it hangs over the violet fabric on one side of the cake and the white on the other. Using scissors, cut the rope so that the ends rest just above the base of the cake.

2 Thinly roll out the deep pink modelling paste and, with a cutting wheel, cut a freehand curvy shape (**F**). Attach over the join between the violet and mid pink fabric at the front of the cake. Make a second and attach to the other edge of the violet fabric.

3 Cut a long, thin pointed strip from thinly rolled lilac paste. Place on the cake so that the paste forms a wave pattern as it falls from the top of the cake. Curl the point up and over where it reaches the board and gather the paste on top of the cake.

LAYER 3

1 Place a little oasis fix into the posy pick and insert the pick into the centre of the cake.

2 Next, make six puffs of fabric in the various colours. Do this by rolling out the modelling paste between the narrow spacers and cutting the paste into rough rectangular or square shapes. Pick up either two or four corners and bring them to the centre (**G**) then arrange the resulting shape over the side of the cake, adjusting the folds as desired (**H**).

LAYER 4

1 Make the ribbon loops by cutting out two 16 x 2cm (6¼ x ¾in) strips from thinly rolled deep pink flowerpaste. Press the ends of each strip together to form loops and place on their sides to dry partially.

2 Add a couple of fabric roses, some silver dragées and a couple of loops of sugar rope on top of the puffs at the back and sides of the cake.

3 Create three or four more puffs to fill the space between layer 3 and the posy pick.

4 Attach the prepared loops and large fabric rose to the top of the cake then add a cluster of silver dragées, as seen in the main picture.

♥ FINISHING TOUCHES ♥

1 Take three lengths of silver jewellery wire and hold one end. With the help of a pair of pliers, bend the wires into a scroll shape to reflect the centre of the fabric rose (**I**). Insert the wires into the posy pick.

2 Attach the ribbon around the edge of the board using the glue stick. Attach the diamanté trim, using jewel glue and pins to hold it in place whilst the glue dries (**J**).

Cup cakes

Cover each cup cake with a disc of white sugarpaste and decorate each with a fabric rose, a selection of fabrics and dragées, as used for the main cake.

Dress it up

♥ Add texture to the fabric using embossers or textured rolling pins.

♥ For a larger occasion, add another cake column underneath, as used for Exquisite Bouquet on page 94.

♥ Paint patterns on the fabric using edible paste colours mixed with clear spirit.

♥ Add edible lustre dusts to give your cake sparkle.

♥ Try adding beads or diamanté to the wires, or feathers to the top.

Dress it down

♥ Use fewer layers, or make the layers in just one colour and white, and add lustre dusts to make it more delicate and interesting.

♥ Omit the ropes.

Baby's Blanket

A dear little boy's face peeps out from a soft blanket on this sensitively made christening cake. The patchwork quilt covering for the sides, with its embossed design of nursery shapes, finishes the cake perfectly. The child's face is formed using a mould, and the skin, eyes and the hair colour can be made to match the baby's own. Of course, the cake can also be easily adapted for a little girl: use pinks and lilacs for the patchwork and make a pink blanket. For a simpler cake see the variation – Cheeky Baby.

Materials

- ♥ modelling paste: 200g (7oz) flesh, 50g (2oz) pale yellow, 225g (8oz) blue, 50g (2oz) pale blue, 50g (2oz) peach, 50g (2oz) pale green
- ♥ white vegetable fat (shortening)
- ♥ dry spaghetti
- ♥ sugarpaste (rolled fondant): 1.2kg (2lb 10oz) ivory
- ♥ 20cm (8in) round cake (see pages 8–11)
- ♥ 1 quantity buttercream, or marzipan and apricot glaze (see pages 14–15)

- ♥ paste colours for painting the baby's face, such as peach, blue or brown, pink, white and black (see Flesh Tones, below)
- ♥ confectioners' glaze
- ♥ sugar glue

Commercially made flesh-coloured modelling paste saves the hassle of mixing your own.

Equipment

- ♥ baby head mould (HP)
- ♥ 'U' tool (PME)
- ♥ Dresden tool
- ♥ glass-headed dressmakers' pin
- ♥ 28cm (11in) round cake drum (board)
- ♥ small palette knife
- ♥ smoother
- ♥ nursery embossers (PC Make a Cradle set)
- ♥ waxed paper
- ♥ patchwork squares set (PC)
- ♥ paintbrushes
- ♥ small rolling pin
- ♥ narrow spacers made from 1.5mm (¹⁄₁₆in) thick card

- ♥ cutting wheel
- ♥ pan scourer
- ♥ craft knife
- ♥ sugar shaper with medium round disc
- ♥ blue ribbon and non-toxic glue stick

If you don't have a baby head mould, make your own using a baby doll's face and moulding gel.

Preparation

♥ BABY'S HEAD ♥

Flesh Tones

For different flesh tones, start with light flesh colour modelling paste, then for:

- ♥ **Black skin:** add brown until the colour is as dark as required, and then add green to obtain the correct skin tone.
- ♥ **Asian skin:** add brown to darken, and blue to obtain the skin tone.
- ♥ **Far Eastern skin:** add yellow and green.

1 Knead some flesh-coloured modelling paste, adding a trace of white vegetable fat. Roll a 3.5cm (1⅜in) ball, roll it into a cone and press the point of the cone firmly into the nose of the baby head mould (**A**). Shape the back of the head, but don't worry about any marks in the paste, as the blanket will cover these. Remove the head from the mould. You can use the head as it comes straight out of the mould, but to make the baby more endearing adjust the features as follows:

2 Open the baby's mouth by holding a 'U' tool at an angle to the face and pulling the bottom lip down fractionally (**B**).

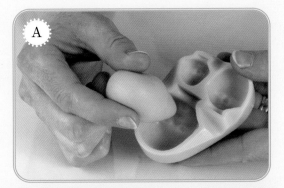

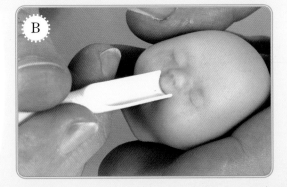

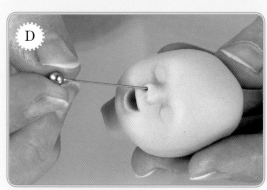

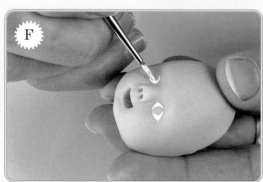

3 Take a Dresden tool and use to enlarge the mouth cavity and restore the corners of the mouth to their correct position to make a smile (**C**).

4 Insert a pin into a nostril and gently circle it to enlarge, and then pull down to the outside (**D**). Repeat for the other nostril.

5 Once you are happy with the shape of the baby's head, cut off the neck and insert a short length of dry spaghetti. Leave to dry. Remove the spaghetti before the paste dries completely.

> An airing cupboard is an excellent place to dry sugar models.

♥ BABY'S BODY ♥

Knead some flesh-coloured modelling paste and roll into a 2.25cm (⅞in) wide 5cm (2in) long sausage. Shape one end into a neck and insert a length of dry spaghetti through the length of the body, leaving some protruding from the neck to support the head later. Leave to dry thoroughly.

Stage One

♥ COVERING THE BOARD ♥

Roll out some of the sugarpaste and use to cover the cake drum. Trim the edges flush with the sides of the board using a small palette knife, taking care to keep the cut vertical. Position the smoother vertically against the edge of the board and then place the teddy embosser from the Make a Cradle set, up against the smoother and press it into the soft paste (**E**). Repeat at regular intervals around the board and leave to dry.

♥ COVERING THE CAKE ♥

1 Place the cake on waxed paper and either cover with apricot glaze and marzipan, if using a fruit cake, or a thin layer of buttercream, if using a sponge cake.

2 Knead the remaining sugarpaste, and then roll it out and use to cover the cake. Smooth the cake by firstly using a smoother to iron out any irregularities in the surface of the icing and then using the base of your hand to smooth and polish the top edge.

3 Take the patchwork square grid embosser and, positioning one long edge at the base of the cake, gently rock the embosser around the side of the cake so that the squares are embossed into the soft paste. Remove the embosser and reposition it so that the lines join up smoothly with the first set, and repeat. Continue until embossed squares encircle the cake. Allow the sugarpaste to dry (see picture **L**).

♥ PAINTING THE BABY'S FACE ♥

1 To paint the face, dilute suitable paste colours in clear spirit and use a fine paintbrush to paint the detail.

2 For the eyes, start by painting the whites (**F**). Then paint the background colour of the iris a pale brown or pale blue. Add details to the iris, such as a dark rim around the outside. Paint the pupil in the centre of the eye; remember that large pupils look more endearing. Allow the paste colours to dry.

> Personalize your baby by changing the hair and eye colour as appropriate.

> Have a detailed look at the baby's eyes you are trying to represent, as all eyes are different.

3 With a fine paintbrush, paint eyelashes, eyebrows and lips using suitable paste colours.

4 Paint over each eye with confectioners' glaze to make the eyes reflective, and then add small white light spots to each, making sure they are in the same position on each eye.

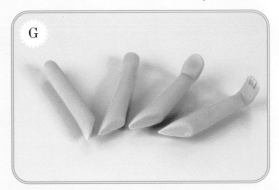

Stage Two

♥ ASSEMBLING THE BABY ♥

1 For the legs, roll an 8mm (⁵⁄₁₆in) wide sausage of flesh modelling paste. Make a cut diagonally across the paste to give two lengths, each measuring 5.5cm (2¼in). Shape the ankle by rolling and thinning the paste between your fingers. Form the foot by squeezing the paste to form the toes and pinching it to form the heel. Then take a pair of scissors and make four small cuts to form five toes (**G**). Sit the body of the baby upright on a board covered in waxed paper and attach the legs to either side with sugar glue.

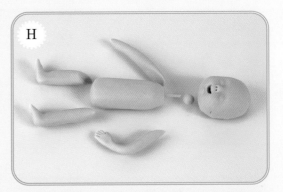

2 For the arms, roll a sausage as for the legs, and cut in two as before. Attach the right arm to the body (this arm will not be seen, so it does not need a hand). Take the left arm and roll and thin the paste to shape the wrist, and then flatten the hand by pinching it. Next, with a pair of small scissors, cut out a small triangle to form the thumb and then make three small cuts to make four fingers (**H**). Attach to the body, bending the arm across the body so that the thumb is uppermost.

3 To create the hair, thinly roll out some pale yellow modelling paste using a small rolling pin, and then take a cutting wheel and run it backwards and forwards over the paste to create thin triangular shapes (**I**). Pick up one section of hair and attach to the top of the baby's head with sugar glue.

4 Create a neck by rolling a pea-sized ball of flesh modelling paste and placing it over the protruding spaghetti, then attach the completed head to the neck using sugar glue.

5 For the blanket, roll out the blue modelling paste between the narrow spacers and cut into a 12 x 23cm (4¾ x 9in) rectangle. Round the corners with a cutting wheel. Take a pan scourer and, pressing firmly and evenly, texture the blue paste (**J**).

6 Carefully lift up the paste and flip it over, then turn over one long edge to give a smooth fold. Drape this fold over the baby's head and arrange the blanket so that it looks soft and natural. Lift the baby's left hand over the blanket's edge and arrange the blanket so that the hand can just be seen. Tuck under the cut edges of blanket, ensuring that the feet are visible.

Try experimenting with different pan scourers to see which textures you prefer.

♥ DECORATING THE CAKE ♥

1 Carefully lift the cake from its waxed paper and place centrally on the prepared cake board.

2 Roll out one of the modelling pastes between the narrow spacers. Emboss the paste with the square grid embosser then add a pattern to the resulting squares using either one of the patchwork squares or nursery embossers (**K**). Repeat for the other colours of modelling pastes using different embossers each time.

3 Neatly separate the squares by cutting along their edges with a palette or craft knife then, using sugar glue, attach the squares to the cake (**L**). Try to position them so that they sit directly over the embossed grid with the colours randomly but evenly spaced.

4 Soften some pale yellow modelling paste. Do this by firstly kneading in some white vegetable fat to stop the paste becoming sticky and then partially dunk the paste into a small container of boiled water before kneading again (the paste should have the consistency of chewing gum). Place the softened paste with the medium round disc into the sugar shaper and squeeze out a length around the base of the cake and another around the top of the patchwork pattern (**M**). Neaten the joins.

5 Attach the baby to the centre of the cake with sugar glue.

6 Using a non-toxic glue stick attach the blue ribbon around the sides of the board to complete the cake (**N**).

If you do not have a sugar shaper you could pipe a border with royal icing or use a bead maker to form two rows of sugar beads.

Dress it up

♥ Add a suitable message or baby's name to the cake using letter cutters.

♥ Model a tiny teddy to sit next to baby, or a little pile of bricks.

Dress it down

♥ Omit the baby and place a gauze fabric bow on the top instead.

♥ Omit the quilt and add baby's name to the side of the cake using large letter cutters.

You could use a range of bright primary colours for the decorations to create a bolder and more vibrant cake with a very different look.

Cheeky Baby

Simplify the baby by adding a fun head rather than a lifelike one. Roll a ball of flesh-coloured modelling paste as before. Holding a suitable cutter at 45 degrees, indent a mouth. (Try out different cutters to create a variety of expressions so that you can see which one you prefer.) Indent eyes with a cocktail stick (toothpick) and add a small ball of paste for a nose. Leave to dry thoroughly before adding small balls of black paste for eyes. The baby can of course be personalized by changing the colour of the hair, and the blanket can be made in any colour.

Golden Wedding

What better way to celebrate a couple's 50th anniversary than this splendid Golden Wedding cake with its ornate 'topper' of gold and ivory hearts? The stacked cake is decorated with scrolls, waves and hearts in modelling paste that are then filled in with swirled gold icing. The swirled theme is reflected in the use of a gold-coloured separator that elevates the top tier giving the design stature and sophistication.

The cake could also easily be adapted for a silver (25 years) or a ruby wedding (40 years).

Make the accompanying cup cakes to match.

Materials

- ♥ cakes: 15cm (6in), 20cm (8in), 25.5cm (10in) round (see pages 8–11)
- ♥ 2 quantities buttercream, or marzipan and apricot glaze (see pages 14–15)
- ♥ sugarpaste (rolled fondant): 3kg (6lb 10oz) ivory
- ♥ golden-brown paste colour
- ♥ gum tragacanth
- ♥ white vegetable fat (shortening)
- ♥ sugar glue
- ♥ royal icing: 3 quantities (add 2.5ml (½ tsp) glycerine per egg to prevent the icing setting too hard)
- ♥ edible gold lustre dust
- ♥ confectioners' glaze

Equipment

- ♥ waxed paper
- ♥ boards: 20cm (8in) round hardboard cake board, 20cm (8in) round cake drum (board) 33cm (13in) round cake drum (board), 10cm (4in) round cake card
- ♥ smoother
- ♥ small palette knife
- ♥ gold heart-shaped cake separator (LC)
- ♥ sugar shaper with small and medium round discs
- ♥ selection of paintbrushes
- ♥ craft knife
- ♥ posy pick
- ♥ set of leaf heart cutters (T)
- ♥ disposable piping bags
- ♥ narrow spacers made from 1.5mm (⅙in) thick card
- ♥ gold 26-gauge straight floristry wires
- ♥ foam
- ♥ topaz matt crystal heart beads (LC)
- ♥ jewel glue, or other clear-drying glue
- ♥ gold ribbon and non-toxic glue stick
- ♥ dowels
- ♥ no. 3 piping tube (tip)
- ♥ glass-headed dressmakers' pin
- ♥ gold bullion wire (LC)
- ♥ a little oasis fix
- ♥ 10cm (4in) circle of non stick matting

You can make your own piping bags from waxed paper.

Stage One

♥ COVERING THE CAKE ♥

1 Place the cakes individually on waxed paper with the 20cm (8in) hardboard cake board under the 20cm (8in) cake. Then cover with apricot glaze and marzipan, if using a fruit cake, or a thin layer of buttercream, if using a sponge cake.

2 Knead 1kg (2¼lb) of sugarpaste to warm it and make it more pliable. Then roll the paste out and use to cover the 25.5cm (10in) cake. Smooth the cake by firstly using a smoother to iron out any irregularities in the surface of the icing, and then using the base of your hand to smooth and polish the top edge. Cover the middle and top tiers in the same way and then set the cakes aside to dry.

♥ COVERING THE BOARDS ♥

1 Colour all but 75g (3oz) of the sugarpaste gold, using the golden-brown paste colour.

2 To mark the separator position on the base of the 20cm (8in) round cake drum, make two paper circles, one by drawing around the board and one by drawing around the separator's base plate. Fold the circles in half and half again to find their centres. Place the 20cm (8in) circle on the underside of the drum and mark the drum's centre with a pin. Remove the larger circle and replace with the smaller. Take a pencil and draw lightly around the edge to mark its position (**A**). Remove and replace with the separator, then firmly draw around its base with a pencil.

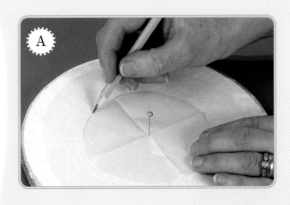

B

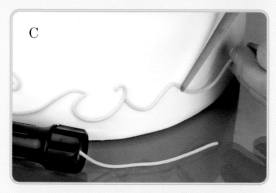

C

D

E

3 Roll out some of the golden-brown sugarpaste and use to cover the larger cake drum. Trim the edges flush with the sides of the board using a small palette knife, taking care to keep the cut vertical. Cover the smaller board and set aside to dry.

♥ MAKING MODELLING PASTE ♥

Mix 25g (1oz) of each of the ivory and gold sugarpastes to make a mid-gold colour. Then add 1.5ml (¼ tsp) of gum tragacanth to make modelling paste. Also add 1.5ml (¼ tsp) of gum tragacanth to 50g (2oz) of gold sugarpaste and the remaining 50g (2oz) of ivory sugarpaste. Leave the modelling paste overnight to mature before using.

Stage Two

♥ ADDING WAVE OUTLINES – BASE AND TOP TIERS ♥

1 Soften some of the gold modelling paste. Do this by firstly kneading in some white vegetable fat to stop the paste becoming sticky and then partially dunk the paste into a small container of boiled water before kneading again (the paste should have the consistency of chewing gum). Place the softened paste with the small round disc into the sugar shaper.

2 Take a fine paintbrush and some sugar glue, and paint a freehand pattern of waves and scrolls around the sides of the base cake (**B**).

3 Squeeze out a length of paste from the sugar shaper (if the paste doesn't come out easily, the paste isn't soft enough) and place it over a section of the painted glue pattern, cut to size on the cake using a palette or craft knife (**C**). Add another length to abut the first and so on until the painted glue pattern is complete.

4 For the top tier, create a wave pattern as for the base tier, but this time create inverted waves (**D**).

♥ ADDING HEART OUTLINES ♥

1 Find the centre of the top tier by folding a 15cm (6in) paper circle in half and half again and placing it on the top of the cake. Mark the centre, where the folds cross, with a pin. Insert a posy pick into the centre of the cake so that it rests fractionally below the surface of the sugarpaste, then place a length of gold modelling paste squeezed from the sugar shaper on top of the edge of the posy pick.

2 Place the smaller leaf heart cutters on top of the cake, and then paint around them with sugar glue. Squeeze out a length of softened modelling paste from the sugar shaper and place around one side of the heart and cut to size. Take a second length and wrap it around the other side of the heart, but this time continue past the point and make a small scroll (**E**). Repeat until you have a random selection of hearts over the top tier.

3 For the base tier, create a few small heart outlines as before, below the line of the waves (see picture below).

♥ FILLING IN THE WAVE PATTERN ♥

1 Colour some of the royal icing in a range of colours from ivory through to gold using the golden-brown paste colour (F). Place each colour separately into a disposable icing bag and cut off the points at the very ends of all the bags.

> Fill the piping bags so that they are only half-full.

2 Choose one of the colours, and squeeze it over a small section under the wave pattern on the base tier, change colours and repeat to create a mottled look (G). Complete only a small section.

3 Add texture to the icing by taking a damp paintbrush and running it through the wet icing to add definition and interest to the pattern.

4 Neaten the base of the cake by removing any excess icing with a damp brush.

5 Continue in sections, adding the icing and texturing, but leaving the leaf hearts empty, until the base tier wave pattern is complete.

6 Cover and texture the top tier in sections as for the base tier. Leave to dry.

♥ DECORATING THE MIDDLE TIER ♥

1 Mark the central position of the separator on the top of the middle tier in the same way as for the 20cm (8in) cake drum.

> Try to avoid getting glue on the separator itself.

2 Attach the 10cm (4in) cake card to the base of the separator using royal icing – it is important that the separator should not stand directly on to the cake. Place the separator in position on the cake and paint a ring of sugar glue on to the cake around the base of the separator.

3 Place some softened gold modelling paste into the sugar shaper with the medium round disc and squeeze out a length around the base of the separator. Cut to size and blend the join, and then remove the separator leaving the modelling paste ring in position.

4 Colour some of the royal icing in a range of colours from ivory through to gold using the golden-brown paste colour. Then, using a palette knife, place some of the icing on to the cake and paddle it slightly to create an interesting texture and shape (H). Change colour and repeat, covering only a small section as before.

5 Take a damp paintbrush and run it through the wet royal icing, to create patterns of swirls and hearts in the icing (I). Neaten the base, as before.

6 Continue adding and texturing the icing in sections until the cake, with the exception of the central circle, is covered. Leave to dry.

♥ MAKING HEART TOPPERS ♥

1 Roll out the three colours of modelling paste between the narrow spacers and cut out a selection of leaf hearts in different sizes. Dip the ends of the floristry wires in sugar glue and insert one into the point of each heart (J). Leave to dry on a flat surface, ideally foam.

2 Take the topaz matt crystal heart beads and, using jewel glue, stick four on to the end of a gold wire, leaving a space of between 1cm (⅜in) and 2cm (¾in) between each bead. Decorate approximately ten wires.

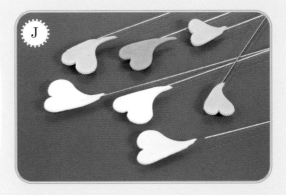

Stage Three

♥ STACKING THE CAKES ♥

1 Remove the base tier from its waxed paper and place it centrally on the prepared cake drum. Add ribbon around the edge of the drum using a glue stick. Repeat for the top tier.

2 Dowel the base tier and the middle tier then attach the middle tier centrally on top of the base tier.

♥ ADDING PIPED HEARTS ♥

To make the small hearts, use gold-coloured royal icing and a no. 3 tube and pipe small 'Y' shapes randomly over the cakes (**K**).

♥ GILDING ♥

Mix some edible gold dust with confectioners' glaze and use to paint over the edges of the wave and scroll pattern (**L**), the piped hearts (**M**) and some of the heart cake toppers. Clean your brush immediately after painting with glaze.

♥ ADDING BULLION WIRE ♥

Place a pin in the base of a cake and wrap the end of the bullion wire around the pin to secure. Unravel and wrap the wire around the cake approximately eight times; do this fairly loosely to give a slight wave effect (**N**). Cut the wire and twist the two ends together. Remove the pin. Note: do not push the ends of the wire into the cake. Repeat for the other tiers.

♥ ARRANGING THE TOPPER ♥

1 Place a small amount of oasis fix into the posy pick to help secure the wires in place.

2 Take a wired heart and gently curve the wire by wrapping it around a cylinder shape, such as a bottle or can (**O**). Cut the wire to an appropriate length for your cake and insert into the posy pick.

3 Create the basic shape of the topper by firstly arranging some curved wired hearts of the same length around the base of the fountain and then using a few straight wired hearts to define the height.

4 Fill in the spaces with the remaining hearts, making sure that they are evenly spaced. Add the wires with the topaz matt crystal heart beads.

It is important that the bullion wire is removed from the cake before it is cut.

5 Finally, take the gold bullion wire and very loosely wrap it around the base of the topper to soften the appearance of the wires. Twist the ends together as before.

♥ ADDING THE SEPARATOR ♥

Using royal icing, stick the 10cm (4in) cake card to the base of the separator, then attach the separator to the middle tier and allow the icing to dry.

Stage Four

♥ ASSEMBLING THE CAKE ♥

Place the non-slip matting on the top plate of the separator and position the top tier, ensuring that the plate of the separator lines up with the drawn circle on the underside of the cake drum. Stand back and admire!

Dress it up

♥ Add another heart separator between the base and middle tier.

Dress it down

♥ This cake has been designed with a large celebration in mind. However, if you are having a small, select gathering, why not just use the top tier?

♥ Remove the separator and have a three-tier stacked cake.

♥ Finish off the cake with a gold sugarpaste rose (see Sumptuous Silk and Exquisite Bouquet on pages 48 and 94) instead of the fountain.

Cup cakes

Cover the top of each cup cake with a disc of ivory sugarpaste. Make the hearts with a sugar shaper and leaf heart cutter as for the top tier, and then add and texture the royal icing around the hearts, as for the main cake. If time is short, why not use modelling paste hearts, as cut for the cake topper, to decorate your cup cakes?

Just Perfect

A single cake for a small gathering will look just as stunning when decorated with its fountain of hearts and beads.

Birthday Butterfly

A small-tortoiseshell butterfly rests on the centre of a giant daisy for this buttercream-covered cake that is simply perfect for a summer birthday or celebration. The crisp white petals are formed from pastillage, and although the cake looks complicated, the individual stages are quite straightforward, and the butterfly can always be simplified if you prefer. Take time to create the butterfly and decorate its wings to achieve the same effect as here, following the design template. Delicate butterfly cup cakes continue the theme.

Materials

- ♥ sugarpaste (rolled fondant): 600g (1lb 5oz) deep blue
- ♥ 15cm (6in) round Madeira or chocolate cake (see pages 8–11)
- ♥ 350g (12oz) pastillage
- ♥ white vegetable fat (shortening)
- ♥ small amount of royal icing
- ♥ 25g (1oz) white modelling paste
- ♥ sugar glue
- ♥ 2 black stamens
- ♥ paste colours: yellow, orange, blue, cream, brown, black
- ♥ clear spirit, such as gin or vodka
- ♥ 1 quantity buttercream
- ♥ liquid colours: yellow and orange (optional)

Save carving by baking your cake in one half of a large ball tin or in an ovenproof pudding bowl.

Equipment

- ♥ 30cm (12in) round cake drum (board)
- ♥ small palette knife
- ♥ thin card
- ♥ 13 cardboard tubes, such as toilet roll tubes
- ♥ waxed paper
- ♥ reusable adhesive
- ♥ narrow spacers made from 1.5mm (⅟₁₆in) thick card
- ♥ cutting wheel
- ♥ craft knife
- ♥ small disposable piping bag made from waxed paper
- ♥ piping tubes (tips) nos 1, 2, 3, 4, 16 and 17
- ♥ glass-headed dressmakers' pin
- ♥ paintbrushes, including a fine one
- ♥ paint palette
- ♥ cocktail stick (toothpick)
- ♥ reusable piping bag and connector
- ♥ blue ribbon and non-toxic glue stick

Preparation

♥ COVERING THE BOARD ♥

Roll out the deep blue sugarpaste and use to cover the cake drum. Trim the edges flush with the sides of the board using a small palette knife, taking care to keep the cut vertical.

♥ PREPARING THE CAKE FOR FREEZING ♥

Level the cake and, if using Madeira, remove the crusts. Freeze overnight.

♥ PASTILLAGE PETALS ♥

1 Transfer the petal template on to a piece of thin card and cover each cardboard tube with waxed paper to make formers. Support the tubes with reusable adhesive (see photo **B**). Smear your work board or work surface with white vegetable fat and roll out some pastillage between the narrow spacers.

2 Place the petal template on the paste and cut around it with a cutting wheel (**A**). Leave the shape for a moment or two before carefully turning it over and placing on a former so that the reverse side is uppermost. This gives a smoother finish to the petals and prevents the white fat from the board sticking the petal to the former (**B**). Make 13 petals, plus some extras to allow for breakages. Allow the petals to dry thoroughly.

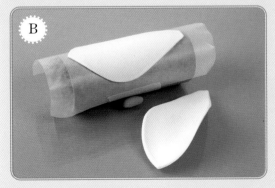

♥ CREATING THE BASIC BUTTERFLY SHAPE ♥

1 Trace the butterfly template on to tracing paper and cut out with sharp scissors. Take a 15 x 10cm (6 x 4in) card and fold in half along the 15cm (6in) edge, place on a flat surface and create the wing former by placing a sausage of reusable adhesive under each wing. Adjust the shape of the card until you are happy with the angle.

2 Roll out some pastillage between narrow spacers, place the butterfly tracing on top, and cut carefully around the template using a cutting wheel on the straight sections and a sharp craft knife along the frilly edges of the wings (**C**). Place the butterfly carefully on the former and leave to dry thoroughly (**D**).

♥ ADDING WING DETAIL ♥

1 Place the butterfly tracing on to the dried wings and, with a pencil, transfer the radial wing markings on to both sides of each wing (**E**).

The lines may be faint, so go over them with a pencil.

2 Half-fill a small piping bag fitted with a no. 1 tube with royal icing. Pipe over the traced lines on the underside of the butterfly and leave to dry. Turn the butterfly over and pipe the lines on the top (**F**). Add extra lines to create the hairs on the lower sections of the wings. Reserve the royal icing for use on the body.

♥ BUTTERFLY'S BODY ♥

Knead the white modelling paste until warm, then, using the butterfly template as a guide, model the three sections of the body as follows (**G**):

1 For the head, roll a very small pea-sized ball. Pinch a small section of the ball and cut the pinched section in two with small scissors to create the mouth piece. Add small balls either side for eyes.

2 To model the thorax, roll a rounded sausage of paste to fit the template, and attach in position with sugar glue to the back of the head.

3 For the abdomen, roll another rounded sausage of modelling paste to fit the template. Take a cutting wheel and indent five lines around the sausage. Attach to the thorax with sugar glue.

4 Create the antennae by firstly using a pin to make a hole either side of the mouth. Then cut the black stamens to length, dip the ends into sugar glue and insert into the prepared holes.

5 Attach the prepared body to the wings, and pipe hairs around the head and thorax of the body as shown.

♥ PAINTING THE BUTTERFLY ♥

1 In a paint palette, separately dilute all the suggested paste colours with clear spirit. Then, using the photographs on this page as a guide, start painting the colours on to the top side of the wings in this order: the yellow patches, the orange sections, with a fine brush the blue crescents, the cream along the edges, followed by the brown on the lower wings and body. Allow these colours to dry thoroughly before adding the final black and grey detail.

2 Once the top is dry, turn the butterfly over and repeat the process for the underside, following the step picture for details of underside markings.

Paint the background colours first before adding the black and grey details.

Painting tips

♥ Make sure the butterfly is completely dry before attempting to paint it.

♥ Painting is a lot easier if you have the right tools, so invest in a selection of good quality paintbrushes.

♥ When painting, use fine strokes with just a small amount of colour on the brush.

♥ Before you add colour to a previously painted area, make sure the first layer is completely dry to avoid accidental smudging.

♥ If pushed for time omit painting the underside of the butterfly, as very little of it will be seen.

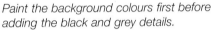

Use fine strokes to give detail to the body and the centre of the wings.

Although it is strong, pastillage is brittle so handle the butterfly and petals with care.

The markings on the underside of the butterfly will not need to be so detailed as they will not be completely visible.

Stage One

♥ CARVING THE CAKE ♥

Mark the centre of the cake with a cocktail stick. Take a sharp knife and carve a curve from the centre of the top of the cake down to the lower rim to create a dome shape (**H**). Remove the cocktail stick.

♥ ASSEMBLING THE FLOWER ♥

Place the carved cake in the centre of the prepared cake board. Take a dried pastillage petal and firmly but carefully insert it under the rim of the dome cake into the sugarpaste below so that it is at a slight angle to the board rather than resting on it (**I**). Repeat for the remaining petals.

♥ FLOWER CENTRE ♥

1 Make one batch of buttercream and divide it into thirds. Then, using liquid colours or paste colours, colour the thirds, yellow, mid orange and deep orange.

2 Using a palette knife, spread a thin coat of deep orange buttercream over the cake to seal in the crumbs.

3 Place a no. 17 tube in a reusable piping bag. Place some of each colour buttercream into the bag and, starting at the base of a petal, squeeze out a slightly elongated dot of icing. (The different shades of buttercream will create a marbled effect.) Repeat around the base of the cake to create a ring. Then pipe an additional five rows of dots up the sides of the cake.

4 Replace the tube with a no. 16 and the icing in the bag with the two lighter colours. Pipe seven rows of dots.

5 Replace the tube with a no. 4 and the icing bag with yellow. Pipe three rows of dots. Then using a no. 3 tube and mid orange icing, pipe another three rows of dots.

6 Finally, fill the centre with deep orange dots piped with a no. 2 tube (**J**). Leave to dry.

Stage Two

♥ ADDING THE BUTTERFLY AND RIBBON ♥

Attach the butterfly to the cake with a small blob of buttercream, and then attach the ribbon around the edge of the cake board using a non-toxic glue stick to complete the cake.

Dress it up

♥ Turn the cake into an engagement or wedding anniversary cake by making two butterflies.

♥ Enlarge the cake to serve more people; for example, use a 20cm (8in) round cake or cook a cake in an ovenproof bowl and make the petals longer.

Dress it down

♥ If you find painting a bit daunting, simplify the butterfly by just painting on a few splashes of colour to create a fantasy butterfly.

♥ Buy a ready-made butterfly and place it on top of the decorated cake.

♥ Omit the butterfly altogether, as the flower by itself makes a lovely cake.

Cup cakes

Using a small butterfly mould (HH), make a selection of butterflies from pastillage, inserting stamens for antennae as above. When dry, paint on the markings of actual butterflies, like these, or make up your own fantasy ones. When the markings have dried, cover the top of each cup cake with a disc of sugarpaste and attach a butterfly to the centre of each with sugar glue.

Fairytale Castle

For a fairytale wedding or a young girl's party, create this towered Fairytale Castle – it could even be made to celebrate moving house. The cakes are covered in sugarpaste and stacked to make a large tiered cake, which is decorated with pastillage and modelling-paste towers. The turrets are simply ice cream cones that have been covered with modelling paste, and edible lustre dusts give them that extra sparkle. If you are adventurous, why not create the variation – Daintily Pink?

Materials

- ♥ sugarpaste (rolled fondant): 4kg (8lb 13oz) ivory
- ♥ cornflour (cornstarch)
- ♥ 2 quantities pastillage
- ♥ white vegetable fat (shortening)
- ♥ sugar glue
- ♥ modelling paste: 875g (1lb 15oz) ivory, 100g (3½oz) gold, 100g (3½oz) lilac

- ♥ cakes: 30cm (12in) round, 25.5cm (10in) (measured point to point) hexagonal, 13cm (5in) round, 10cm (4in) round Madeira or chocolate cakes (see pages 8–11)
- ♥ 2 quantities buttercream
- ♥ a small amount of royal icing, coloured ivory
- ♥ 10 ice cream cones
- ♥ edible dusts: gold lustre, violet sparkle

Mixing cake types
This cake has been made completely from sponge cakes – you can of course vary the type of cake base, but do make allowances if you mix fruit and sponge cakes so that all the elements fit together.

Equipment

- ♥ 40.5cm (16in) round cake drum (board)
- ♥ palette knife
- ♥ cardboard tubes of suitable sizes, such as toilet roll and kitchen roll tubes
- ♥ clear film (plastic wrap)
- ♥ narrow spacers made from 1.5mm (¹⁄₁₆in) thick card
- ♥ craft knife
- ♥ cutters: diamond cutters: 4cm (1½in) and 3cm (1¹⁄₈in) long, circle: 6cm (2³⁄₈in) pastry cutter, shield cutter (FMM, shield 3A), no. 4 straight frill cutter (FMM)
- ♥ foam for drying pastillage discs
- ♥ waxed paper
- ♥ smoother

- ♥ boards: 23cm (9in) round hardboard cake board, 2 x 10cm (4in) round hardboard cake boards
- ♥ dowels
- ♥ cocktail sticks (toothpicks)
- ♥ spirit level
- ♥ piping bag
- ♥ piping tubes (tips), nos 2 and 4
- ♥ paintbrushes
- ♥ sugar shaper with large ribbon, square, medium round and small round discs
- ♥ 5mm (³⁄₁₆in) spacers, made from strip wood
- ♥ multi-ribbon cutter (FMM)
- ♥ straightedge, such as a ruler
- ♥ gold ribbon and gold braid, and non-toxic glue stick

Preparation

♥ COVERING THE BOARD ♥

Roll out some of the sugarpaste and use to cover the cake drum. Trim the edges flush with the sides of the board using a small palette knife. Set aside to dry.

♥ MAKING TOWER 1 ♥

1 Take a small cardboard tube, cover it in clear film then dust with cornflour (**A**).

2 Knead the pastillage to warm it, then roll it out between the narrow spacers, using white fat to prevent it sticking. Cut the paste into a 10cm (4in) wide strip. Place the tube on the pastillage so that one round end of the tube is flush with a cut edge. Roll the tube up in the paste (**B**) and cut away the excess. Stick the join with sugar glue then rub quickly closed. If the pastillage has stretched, trim it back to a height of 10cm (4in) with a palette knife.

3 Take the larger diamond cutter and remove a window from the tower (**C**). When removing windows, check the position of the pastillage join and place the window at 90 degrees to it.

4 Place the tower in a warm, dry place – an airing cupboard is ideal – and leave to dry out completely; allow a few days for this.

The drying process will be speeded up if you carefully remove the tube when the tower is partially dry.

♥ MAKING TOWERS 2–10 ♥

Make the remaining towers as tower 1, but make them to the following heights, and refer to the sketch and photos for window placements:

Tower 2: 10cm (4in)	Tower 7: 13cm (5in)
Tower 3: 19cm (7½in)	Tower 8: 18cm (7in)
Tower 4: 19cm (7½in)	Tower 9: 20cm (8in)
Tower 5: 12cm (4¾in)	Tower 10: 14cm (5½in)
Tower 6: 9cm (3½in)	

♥ MAKING PASTILLAGE DISCS ♥

Roll out the remaining pastillage between the narrow spacers, and cut 11 x 6cm (2⅜in) circles. Place on foam and leave to dry completely.

♥ COVERING THE TOWERS ♥

1 Take one of the completely dried towers. Decide where the join in the paste is to go – ideally in a position that will not be seen on the finished cake – and paint sugar glue down the length of the tower at this point and around the lower and upper edges.

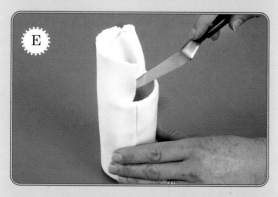

2 Roll out some ivory modelling paste between the narrow spacers and cut one long edge straight. Turn over the modelling paste and, placing the base of the tower on the cut edge, roll up the tower (**D**). Cut the paste to fit, and blend the join as neatly as possible. Trim away the excess paste from the top of the tower with a palette knife (**E**).

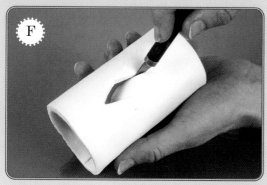

3 Then, with a craft knife, remove the modelling paste from each window, cutting the paste flush with the edge of the pastillage (**F**).

4 Repeat for the remaining towers, and leave to dry.

Stage One

♥ COVERING THE CAKES ♥

1 Level the cakes. Place the 30cm (12in) cake centrally on the previously covered cake drum and the other cakes individually on waxed paper, with the 23cm (9in) hardboard cake board centrally under the hexagonal cake, a 10cm (4in) cake board centrally under the 13cm (5in) cake and the other 10cm (4in) cake board under the 10cm (4in) cake.

2 Cover each with a thin layer of buttercream, taking care not to get any on the covered cake drum.

3 Knead 1.5 kg (3lb 5oz) of ivory sugarpaste to warm it and make it more pliable. Roll the paste out and use to cover the 30cm (12in) cake. Smooth the cake by firstly using a smoother to iron out any irregularities in the surface of the icing and then the base of your hand to smooth and polish the top edge. Cover the remaining cakes and set aside to dry.

If you carefully carve away the very top edge of each cake you will achieve a rounder finish.

Stage Two

♥ STACKING THE CAKE ♥

1 Dowel all the cakes, including the top tier with four dowels per cake (see page 16).

2 Referring to the bird's eye-view sketch, mark the position of the towers on the 13cm (5in) and 30cm (12in) cakes with cocktail sticks. Take the 6cm (⅜in) pastry cutter and, holding the cutter horizontally over one of the tower's positions, push vertically down through the side of the cake to create a recess in which a tower will sit. Check that the appropriate tower sits snugly in the recess, and adjust the cut as necessary. Repeat for the other towers. Finally, stack the cakes.

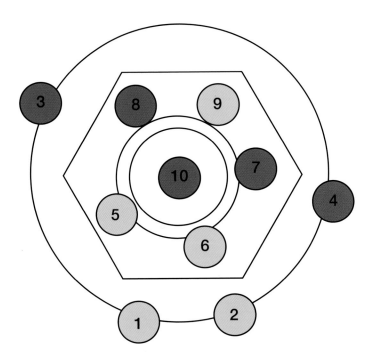

♥ ADDING THE TOWERS ♥

1 Half-fill a piping bag fitted with a no. 4 tube with royal icing. Pipe a line of icing around the base of a tower and position it on the cake. Using a spirit level, ensure the tower sits vertically, adding extra modelling paste to the base to adjust if necessary. Fill the join between the tower and cake with royal icing. Neaten and smooth the icing to shape with a damp paintbrush. Attach all the remaining towers except tower 10.

2 Place one pastillage disc on the top of each tower and attach in place with royal icing. Attach the remaining disc to the base of tower 10. Leave to dry.

3 Take an ice cream cone and cover the rim with royal icing (G), invert and place on the top of a tower. Check that the cone looks vertical, and leave to dry. Attach the remaining cones.

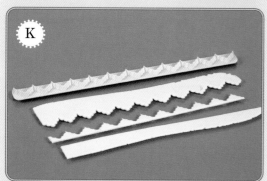

♥ DECORATING THE SPIRES ♥

1 Cover a cone with sugar glue. Soften some gold modelling paste. Do this by firstly kneading in some white vegetable fat to stop the paste becoming sticky, and then partially dunk the paste into a small container of boiled water before kneading again (the paste should have the consistency of chewing gum). Place the softened paste with the large ribbon disc into the sugar shaper, and partially squeeze out a length. Starting at the front of the cone, wrap the resulting ribbon around the cone, working up the cone in a spiral (**H**). Continue squeezing out and wrapping the ribbon until the modelling paste in the sugar shaper has finished. Cut the paste at the back and reload the sugar shaper, continuing up to the top of the cone.

Try to ensure that the ribbon overlaps are as equal as possible.

2 Repeat for the remaining towers, changing to the lilac modelling paste halfway through.

3 To add the shine, firstly, brush over the coloured paste of the spires with white vegetable fat. Next, take a soft-bristled brush and carefully dust the towers, as appropriate, with either the gold lustre dust or the violet sparkle dust.

4 For the spire tops, add 1.5cm (⅝in) wide balls rolled from ivory modelling paste. Top with 6mm (¼in) balls and then pipe a small dot with royal icing using a no. 2 tube (**I**).

♥ DOORWAYS ♥

Roll out some ivory modelling paste between the 5mm (³⁄₁₆in) spacers. Cut out a rectangle to fit between towers 1 and 2. Using the shield cutter, remove a door from the lower edge and attach the paste, minus the door, to the cake. Create the doorway between towers 5 and 6 in the same way, but make this doorway slightly smaller.

If you don't have a shield cutter, cut out the doors by hand using a cutting wheel or craft knife.

♥ PARAPETS ♥

1 Roll out some ivory modelling paste between the narrow spacers, and then, using the multi-ribbon cutter, cut ten 1.25cm (½in) wide strips (**J**). Paint glue over the joins between the tops of the towers and the spires and attach a strip to each of the towers so that the joins are at the back.

2 Roll out some more modelling paste and press the no. 4 straight frill cutter into the paste. Measure 1.25cm (½in) from the top point of the pattern, and using a straightedge, cut the strip to this depth (**K**). Using sugar glue, attach the strip on top of a tower, with the join at the back, encouraging the points of the frill to fall slightly outwards. Repeat for the other towers.

3 Make more parapets, using the straight frill cutter, but this time cut them to a depth of 1.75cm (¾in). Attach around the top of each tier, ensuring that they are placed at the same height all the way round on each layer. Position the points so that they are vertical, and then attach an additional ring of parapets around the base of the top tier.

♥ ROYAL ICING DETAIL ♥

Half-fill a piping bag with royal icing fitted with a no. 2 tube. Pipe small dots at regular intervals under all the parapets, around the base of the bands on the towers and around the doorways (**L**). Also add a dividing line for the main door, and two handles.

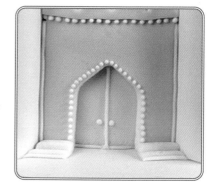

♥ MODELLING-PASTE TRIM ♥

1 Attach tower 10 in position.

2 Soften some ivory modelling paste, as above, and place in the sugar shaper with the square disc. Paint sugar glue around the base of the 30cm (12in) cake, either side of the smaller doorway and around the base of tower 10. Squeeze out lengths of paste and place over the glue.

3 Change the disc to the medium round disc, and squeeze out lengths. Using sugar glue as before, attach these in front of the square trim (**M**), around the base of the hexagonal cake and around the base of the towers and cake on the 13cm (5in) layer.

4 Replace the disc with the small round disc, and squeeze out lengths. Attach these up the sides of each tower where it joins the cake, and around the trim on the base and hexagonal cakes and tower 10.

♥ FINISHING TOUCHES ♥

1 Lightly dust the castle with lustre dusts to add more sparkle.

2 Attach the gold ribbon and braid to the edge of the cake drum using a non-toxic glue stick.

Daintily Pink

You can change the colour scheme, as here, to white, pink and silver, which would particularly appeal to a little girl who loves all things pink. The decoration can be embellished by adding small, cut-out flowers and diamonds and piped dots of royal icing, with silver dragées (sugar balls) for added detail.

Dress it up

♥ Add the inverted frill as shown in Daintily Pink, and inset it with cut-out flowers in lilac and gold.

♥ Add a row of cut-out flowers in-between the lines of piped dots on the towers.

♥ Pipe around the windows with royal icing.

♥ Paint the doors with gold paste colours and lustre dusts.

Dress it down

♥ Reduce the number of towers.

♥ Remove a tier from the cake.

Klimt Inspiration

Gustav Klimt (1862–1918) painted some intricate and decorative paintings, which often contained highly patterned gold areas. This wedding cake echoes his lavish use of gold and geometric ornamentation by creating bold patterns for each tier and topping the ball cake on the upper tier with curved gold wires and beads. Although the finished effect is stunning and appears ambitious, with care you will be able to reproduce the effect fairly easily. There are also some ornamented cup cakes to partner the cake.

Materials

- sugarpaste (rolled fondant): 1kg (2¼lb) blue, 800g (1¾lb) gold (to match the edible gold lustre dust), 600g (1lb 5oz) cream
- paste colours: bright turquoise blue, mid blue
- clear spirit, such as gin or vodka
- cakes: 20cm (8in) round cake, 15cm (6in) (measured point to point) hexagonal cake, 10cm (4in) ball cake (see pages 8–11)
- 1 quantity buttercream, or marzipan and apricot glaze (see pages 14–15)

- modelling paste: 50g (2oz) blue, 50g (2oz) gold, 50g (2oz) ivory
- edible gold lustre dust
- confectioners' glaze
- sugar glue
- white vegetable fat (shortening)

> If you don't have a ball tin, use a polystyrene (styrofoam) ball instead as a dummy.

Equipment

- boards: 28cm (11in) (measured side to side) hexagonal cake drum (board), 13cm (5in) round hardwood cake board, 7.5cm (3in) cake card
- small palette knife
- stippling brush and paintbrushes, including flat-headed
- waxed paper
- smoother
- cutting wheel
- cutters: circles: 1.5cm (⅝in), 1cm (⅜in), 8mm (⅝in) (no. 18 PME tube), 6mm (¼in) (no. 17 PME tube), 4mm (⅛in) (no. 4 PME tube); long teardrops: 2.25cm (⅞in) and 1.75cm (¾in); 2cm (¾in) square; set of small equilateral triangles, side measurements: 3.25cm (1¼in), 2.5cm (1in), 1.5cm (⅝in), 1.25cm (½in)

- cocktail stick (toothpick)
- dowels
- narrow spacers made from 1.5mm (1/16in) thick card
- glass-headed dressmakers' pins
- sugar shaper with medium round and medium ribbon discs
- posy pick
- a little oasis fix
- craft knife
- gold metallic reel wire or 0.6mm jewellery wire
- 1.5cm (⅝in) wide tube or pencil for coiling the wire
- wire clippers
- 6mm (¼in) blue glass pearls
- blue ribbon and gold braid, and non-toxic glue stick

> Piping tubes make perfect cutters for small circles.

Preparation

♥ THE BOARD ♥

1 Roll out the blue sugarpaste and use to cover the cake drum. Trim the edges flush with the sides of the board using a small palette knife. Set aside to dry.

2 Once dry, dilute the two paste colours separately in clear spirit. Take a stippling brush and stipple the edge of the covered board with the bright turquoise (**A**), and then change to the mid blue and stipple inside the turquoise. Clean and dry the brush, and then stipple over the join between the two colours to blend (**B**). Take a paintbrush and paint the vertical sugarpaste edge to the board with the diluted bright turquoise.

Stage One

♥ COVERING THE CAKES ♥

1 To cover the round cake, place the cake on waxed paper and cover as appropriate, with buttercream or apricot glaze and marzipan. Roll out the gold-coloured sugarpaste and use to cover the cake. Smooth the cake by firstly using a smoother to iron out any irregularities in the surface of the icing and then the base of your hand to smooth and polish the top edge. Remove the excess paste from the base. Take the small end of the cutting wheel and carefully run the wheel over the paste in a freehand wavy line, taking care to press only halfway through the paste. Repeat at intervals around the cake, bringing the lines up over the top of the cake (**C**).

2 Indent a circle inside each wave (**D**) using the 1cm (⅜in), 6mm (¼in) and 4mm (⅛in) circle cutters. With a cocktail stick make a hole in the centre of each. Set the cake aside to dry.

3 For the hexagonal cake, place the cake centrally on the 13cm (5in) round hardwood cake board then stand it on waxed paper. Insert three dowels into the central area of the cake and place the 7.5cm (3in) cake card on top. Cover the cake with buttercream or apricot glaze and marzipan, depending on the type of cake base you are using. Then cover the cake with cream sugarpaste and set aside to dry.

4 For the ball cake, place the cake on waxed paper and cover with buttercream or marzipan. Roll out the blue sugarpaste and place over the ball cake. Ease it around the base of the cake and pull up the excess paste to form one or two pleats. Cut the pleat(s) away with scissors and smooth the join(s) closed, they should disappear quite readily with the heat of your hand. Trim the excess paste away from the base of the cake. Next, using a smoother and then your hand, smooth the surface of the cake with vertical strokes. Leave to dry.

> It is worth spending time doing this; the paste will not dry out if you continually work it.

♥ MAKING THE BLUE CIRCLES ♥

Roll out the blue modelling paste between the narrow spacers and cut out a selection of about 35–40 circles using the suggested sizes; include at least six 1.5cm (⅝in) circles for the middle tier. Place on waxed paper and set aside to dry.

Stage Two

♥ PAINTING THE CAKES ♥

1 Mix the edible gold lustre dust with some confectioners' glaze. Take a flat-headed brush and, using vertical sweeping strokes, apply two layers of gold paint to the surface of the round cake (**E**).

2 Once the sugarpaste on the ball cake has crusted over, dilute the two paste colours separately in clear spirit. Bring the waxed paper, on which the ball cake is sitting, over the edge of your work board or work surface and stipple the underside of the ball with the mid blue colour. Stipple halfway up the ball before changing to the turquoise and painting over the top. Blend the colours as for the board. Leave to dry.

> When using glaze, remember to clean your brush immediately after use.

3 Paint each of the prepared blue circles with the diluted turquoise and mid-blue paste colours and leave to dry.

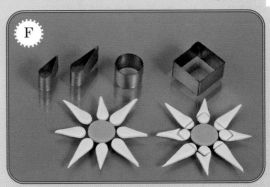

♥ STAR DECORATION ♥

Roll out the gold modelling paste between the narrow spacers, and cut out four large teardrops and four small teardrops. Place a 1.5cm (⅝in) blue circle on waxed paper and arrange the teardrops around the circle as shown (**F**). Take the square cutter and place it centrally over the circle, adjusting the position of the teardrops as necessary. Press down on the cutter, then remove the small pieces of excess paste from the middle. Make five more stars and leave to dry.

Stage Three

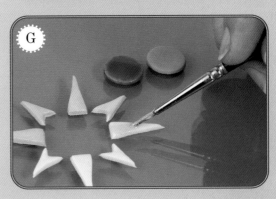

♥ DECORATING THE HEXAGONAL TIER ♥

1 Mix some edible gold lustre dust with confectioners' glaze, and gild the stars (**G**).

2 To make a template for the side of the hexagonal cake, cut some greaseproof paper the length and height of one side. Find the centre by folding the paper in half and half again, and then draw around the square cutter placed over the centre.

3 Place the template on one side of the cake and insert pins in each corner of the square (**H**). Remove the pins and repeat for the other sides.

4 Using sugar glue and the pin marks for guidance, attach the star to the cake (**I**), and then finish off with a blue circle in the centre.

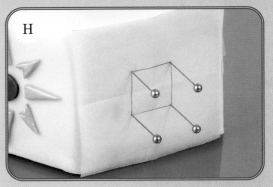

♥ ASSEMBLING THE CAKE ♥

1 Place the round cake centrally on the prepared board. Dowel the round cake and place the hexagonal cake on top. Then attach the ball cake to the top of the hexagonal cake.

2 Soften some ivory modelling paste. Do this by firstly kneading in some white vegetable fat to stop the paste becoming sticky and then partially dunk the paste into a small container of boiled water before kneading again (the paste should have the consistency of chewing gum). Place the softened paste with the medium round disc into the sugar shaper, and squeeze out a length around the base of the round cake and the base of the ball cake. Neaten the join.

3 Soften some blue modelling paste, and place in the sugar shaper with the medium ribbon disc. Squeeze out a length around the base of the hexagonal tier (**J**).

♥ DECORATING THE BALL CAKE ♥

1 Insert a posy pick into the top of the ball cake. Place a small amount of oasis fix into the pick to help hold the wires of the topper securely. To make arranging the wires easier it is worth spending time ensuring the posy pick is inserted vertically into the cake.

2 Roll out some gold modelling paste between the narrow spacers, and cut out six of the largest and small circles and 12 of all the other sizes. Place the circles on waxed paper and, while they are still soft, paint them with gold lustre dust mixed with confectioners' glaze, as for the stars and base cake.

3 Roll out some ivory modelling paste between the narrow spacers and cut out six of the largest triangles, then 12 of all the other sizes. Then cut six more with 8mm (⅝in) length sides (use a craft knife to cut a larger triangle to size).

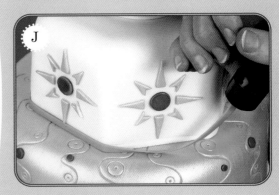

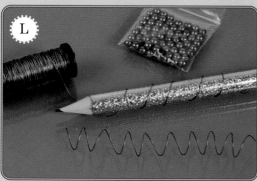

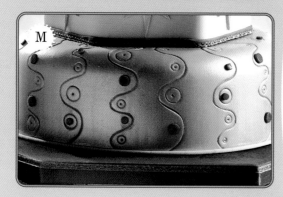

4 Arrange the 8mm (⁵⁄₁₆in) triangles around the posy pick so that they are an equal distance apart and point down to the centre of each side of the hexagon. Add triangles of the next size up to the point of the smallest, and so on until you have created six graduated columns of triangles (see picture **K**).

5 Add the gold circles, their paste should still be soft, to the centres of the triangles (**K**).

♥ WIRE TOPPER ♥
Take the gold wire and coil it around the tube or pencil to create a spring effect that repeats the pattern on the gold tier of the cake (**L**). Cut the spring to approximately 12cm (4¾in) in length with wire clippers, and then thread a couple of blue glass pearls on to the wire and insert into the posy pick. Repeat until you are happy with the effect you have created.

♥ FINISHING TOUCHES ♥
1 Attach the painted blue circles to the base tier.

2 Attach a blue ribbon and gold braid to the edge of the board and gold braid on top of the blue band on the middle tier (**M**).

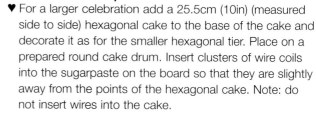

Dress it up
♥ For a larger celebration add a 25.5cm (10in) (measured side to side) hexagonal cake to the base of the cake and decorate it as for the smaller hexagonal tier. Place on a prepared round cake drum. Insert clusters of wire coils into the sugarpaste on the board so that they are slightly away from the points of the hexagonal cake. Note: do not insert wires into the cake.

♥ Use a swirl cake separator (LC) to add height and impact to the cake. The shape of the separator reflects the wave pattern of the gold tier and coils of the wires. (There are also many other separator designs available for you to experiment with.)

Dress it down
♥ Make a two-layer cake using the ball and the lower tier.

♥ Use straight wires with a bead, or omit the wires entirely.

♥ Use the swirling line design for the centre cake and add gold-painted circles to contrast with the blue and gold lower tier, or leave without the added circles.

Cup cakes
Cover the top of each cup cake with a disc of blue sugarpaste. Paint over the sugarpaste to intensify the blue, and leave to dry. Make triangles and gold circles as for the ball cake and attach with sugar glue. Alternatively, use the star design from the hexagonal cake.

Elegance

For a larger celebration, make this splendid version of Klimt Inspiration that is sure to stand out in the crowd. Use a separator and an additional tier (in this case a larger lower tier) to add extra servings and increase the height.

Extra decoration added to the bottom of a very tall cake, such as the wire and beads added here, will help to balance the look of the cake, and make sure that eyes are drawn to every part of your creation.

Fun Flowers

Here's a brightly coloured and boldly decorated cake that would make a great birthday cake for a fun-loving person. It would also make a different and striking wedding cake. The painted effect is achieved by stippling paste colours on to pale yellow sugarpaste, and bright cut-out flowers complete the sunny appearance. If you prefer a quieter tone to your cake, you could change the colours, perhaps using soft pastel shades. For an even wilder occasion, however, try the variation – Crazy Colours.

Materials

- ♥ sugarpaste (rolled fondant): 600g (1lb 5oz) pink, 1.2kg (2lb 10oz) ivory, 600g (1lb 5oz) yellow
- ♥ paste colours: rose/ruby, yellow, orange
- ♥ clear spirit, such as gin or vodka
- ♥ cakes: 10cm (4in), 15cm (6in), 20cm (8in) round cakes (see pages 8–11)
- ♥ 1 quantity buttercream, or marzipan and apricot glaze (see pages 14–15)
- ♥ black edible dust colour
- ♥ confectioners' glaze
- ♥ modelling paste: 50g (2oz) deep pink, 50g (2oz) ivory, 15g (½oz) black, 50g (2oz) yellow
- ♥ sugar glue
- ♥ white vegetable fat (shortening)

Equipment

- ♥ boards: 28cm (11in) round cake drum (board), 15cm (6in) round hardboard cake board, 10cm (4in) round hardboard cake board or cake card
- ♥ small palette knife
- ♥ paintbrushes and a stippling brush
- ♥ waxed paper
- ♥ smoother
- ♥ 10 x 20-gauge white wire
- ♥ narrow spacers made from 1.5mm (⅟₁₆in) thick card
- ♥ cutters: five-petal blossom cutter (FMM), small pointed oval, circle: 7cm (2¾in), 4.5cm (1¾in), 3cm (1¼in), 7mm (⁹⁄₃₂in) (no. 18 tube), and 5mm (³⁄₁₆in) (no. 16 tube)
- ♥ Dresden tool
- ♥ CelPad (optional)
- ♥ ball tool
- ♥ daisy centre moulds (JEM) (optional)
- ♥ foam, for drying
- ♥ deep pink and orange ribbons, and non-toxic glue stick
- ♥ dowels
- ♥ craft knife
- ♥ multi-ribbon cutter
- ♥ 3mm (⅛in) wide strip cutter (JEM)
- ♥ sugar shaper with small round disc
- ♥ posy pick
- ♥ a little oasis fix

Preparation

♥ THE BOARD ♥

Roll out the pink sugarpaste and use to cover the cake drum. Trim the edges flush with the sides of the board using a palette knife, taking care to keep the cut vertical. Set aside to dry.

Stage One

♥ PAINTING THE BOARD ♥

Dilute the rose/ruby paste colour in clear spirit. Take a stippling brush and stipple the edge of the covered board (**A**). Take a paintbrush and paint the vertical sugarpaste edge to the board with the diluted paste colour. Leave to dry thoroughly.

♥ COVERING THE CAKE ♥

1 Place the cakes individually on waxed paper with the hardboard cake boards under the smaller cakes. Cover with apricot glaze and marzipan, if using fruit cakes, or a thin layer of buttercream if using sponge cakes.

2 Knead 900kg (2lb) of ivory sugarpaste to warm it and make it more pliable. Then roll the paste out and use to cover the 20cm (8in) cake. Smooth the cake by firstly using a smoother to iron out any irregularities in the surface of the icing and then using the base of your hand to smooth and polish the top edge. Cover the 10cm (4in) cake with the remaining ivory sugarpaste, then cover the 15cm (6in) cake with the yellow sugarpaste. Set the cakes aside to dry.

♥ PAINTING THE WIRES BLACK ♥

Mix the black dust with confectioners' glaze and use to paint the white wires black. Leave to dry. Clean your brush immediately.

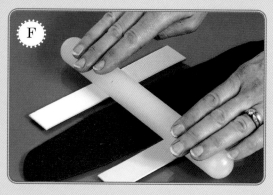

Stage Two

♥ PAINTING THE MIDDLE TIER ♥

Dilute each of the yellow and orange paste colours separately in clear spirit. Take a stippling brush and stipple the top and three-quarters of the way down the sides of the middle tier with yellow paste colour (**B**), and then change to the orange and stipple over the edge of the yellow down to the base. Clean and dry the brush, and then stipple over the line between the two colours to blend the join.

♥ ADDING GLAZE TO THE BOARD ♥

Stipple over the board with confectioners' glaze to make the board reflective. Remember to clean your brush immediately.

♥ MAKING THE FLOWER TOPPERS ♥

1 Roll out the pink and ivory modelling paste between the narrow spacers. Then, using the five-petal blossom cutter, cut out five of each colour. Press the pointed end of a Dresden tool between each petal and drag the paste towards the middle to create more rounded petals (**C**).

2 Place the flower on a CelPad or in the palm of your hand. Press into the centre of each petal with the small end of the ball tool to create a cupped effect (**D**).

3 Make centres by pressing a small ball of yellow modelling paste into a daisy centre mould (**E**). Alternatively, roll balls of paste by hand and cut in half.

4 Attach the centres, then dip one end of each wire into sugar glue and insert a wire into the side of each flower between two petals. Leave to dry horizontally, ideally on foam.

Stage Three

♥ STACKING THE CAKES ♥

1 Remove the base tier from its waxed paper and place it centrally on the prepared cake drum. Add the ribbons around the edge of the drum using a glue stick.

2 Dowel the base tier and the middle tier (see page 16), and then attach the middle tier centrally on top of the base tier and the top tier centrally on to the middle tier.

♥ ADDING PINK STRIPS ♥

1 Knead the pink modelling paste to warm it, and then roll it into a sausage and flatten it with a rolling pin. Place between the narrow spacers and roll the paste to the desired thickness (**F**).

2 Using a multi-ribbon cutter, cut out two 1.3cm (½in) wide strips (**G**), and place one vertically around the base of the middle tier and the other horizontally around the base of the top tier.

♥ DECORATING THE BASE AND TOP TIER ♥

1 Roll out the yellow modelling paste between the narrow spacers, and cut out petals using the pointed oval cutter, and centres with the no. 16 tube (**H**). Using a paintbrush previously dipped in sugar glue, stick the petals and centres to the cakes (**I**), referring to the main picture for placement.

2 Roll out some ivory modelling paste into a long strip. Add textured parallel lines across the strip by repeatedly pressing on to the strip with the 3mm (⅛in) strip cutter, taking care not to press all the way through. Cut a 1.3cm (½in) strip using the multi-ribbon cutter, and attach vertically around the top tier. Cut a further strip, this time to a width of 1.5cm (⅝in) and attach vertically to the base tier.

3 Colour 25g (1oz) of yellow modelling paste orange. Roll out between the narrow spacers and cut the strip lengthways, using the 3mm (⅛in) strip cutter, this time pressing the cutter all the way through the paste (**J**). Cut the strips into 2.5cm (1in) lengths for the base tier and 1.75cm (¾in) lengths for the top tier. Fold each length in half and attach one length on to every fourth ridge of the ivory strip (**K**).

♥ DECORATING THE MIDDLE TIER ♥

1 Make pink and ivory flowers, as for the topper, and attach alternately around the sides of the middle tier.

2 Soften the black modelling paste. Do this by firstly kneading in some white vegetable fat to stop the paste becoming sticky and then partially dunking the paste into a small container of boiled water before kneading again (the paste should have the consistency of chewing gum). Place the softened paste with the small round disc into the sugar shaper. Take a fine paintbrush and some sugar glue, and paint curved stems on all the flowers, referring to the main picture. Squeeze out a length of paste from the sugar shaper (if the paste does not come out easily, the paste is not soft enough) and place it over a painted glue stem; cut the stem to size. Repeat.

If you do not have a sugar shaper, roll the stems by hand.

3 Using the pointed oval cutter, cut ivory leaves from thinly rolled modelling paste. Attach to some of the stems.

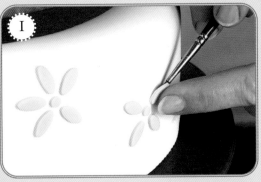

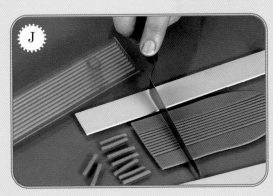

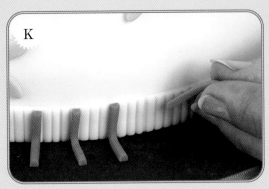

♥ TOP TIER CIRCLE DECORATION ♥

1 Find the centre of the top tier by folding a 10cm (4in) paper circle in half and half again, and placing it on the top of the cake. Mark the centre, where the folds cross, with a pin (**L**). Insert a posy pick vertically into the centre of the cake so that it is flush with the surface of the sugarpaste (**M**).

2 Roll out the pink, ivory and yellow modelling pastes between narrow spacers. Cut a 7cm (2¾in) pink circle, a 4.5cm (1¾in) ivory circle and a 3cm (⅛in) yellow circle. Mark the centre of each using a paper template as above. Then remove a circle from the centre of the ivory and yellow circles the same size as the diameter of your posy pick (you can use a no. 18 tube) and a 4.5cm (1¾in) circle from the pink circle. Place the ivory circle on the cake, centring it over the posy pick. Add the yellow circle on top and the pink around the sides.

3 Finish off the top by adding orange strips in a radial pattern around the yellow circle.

♥ ARRANGING THE TOPPER ♥

1 Place a small amount of oasis fix into the posy pick to help secure the wires in place.

2 Take a wired flower and gently curve the wire to shape. Cut to an appropriate length and insert into the posy pick.

3 Create the basic shape of the topper, and then infill with the remaining flowers.

Crazy Colours

The colour scheme of this cake can easily be varied (have a look at the colour scheme section on page 19–21 if you are stuck for ideas). This blue variation makes a striking cake and could be used with the yellow tier if you wanted something eye-catching for a larger gathering. Be as bold as you dare!

Dress it up

♥ Add another tier so that the cake serves more people by repeating the middle tier decoration on a 25.5cm (10in) cake.

♥ For a fun wedding cake, add a fourth and fifth tier. Replace the wired flowers with a modelled bride and groom (see Pink Sparkle on page 88).

♥ Decorate two tiers of the cake in the same way as the decoration for the middle tier (with yellow and orange painting and red and white flowers) and make the middle a white tier with yellow flowers.

Dress it down

♥ Use either one or two tiers of the design.

♥ Omit the yellow and orange painting stage from the middle tier.

♥ Omit the orange trim.

♥ Omit the topper.

Flower Power

Simply add another coordinating tier to the cake if you are making the cake for a large event where you want to serve more people. See 'Dress it up', above, for details.

Pink Sparkle

Silver, pink and white make a delicate colour theme for this attractive two-tiered wedding cake that is quite simple to create. A petal-shaped cake used for the top contributes to the soft effect, accentuated by the use of silver balls and heart dragées. The figures can be personalized simply by matching the hair and skin and clothes to the couple's own. The matching cup cakes are sure to be especially popular with younger guests.

Materials

- sugarpaste (rolled fondant): 700g (1½lb) deep pink, 600g (1lb 5oz) pale pink, 900g (2lb) white
- white vegetable fat (shortening)
- cakes: 23cm (9in) round and 15cm (6in) petal (see pages 8–11)
- buttercream and/or apricot glaze and marzipan (for fruit cakes) (see pages 14–15)
- modelling paste: 75g (3oz) white, 50g (2oz) flesh, 50g (2oz) black, 25g (1oz) dark grey, 15g (½oz) brown, 15g (½oz) pink

- sugar glue
- spaghetti
- dragées (sugar balls): 25g (1oz) 4mm (⅛in) silver balls, 15g (½oz) 4mm (⅛in) pink balls, a few 6mm (¼in) silver balls, a few 8–10mm (⅜–⅝in) silver balls
- pink dust colour
- small amount of royal icing
- 150g (5oz) 1cm (⅜in) silver heart-shaped dragées
- silver dust colour
- confectioners' glaze

Equipment

- boards: 33cm (13in) round cake drum (board)
- 13cm (5in) round hardboard cake board
- waxed paper
- smoother
- paintbrushes
- cutters: 2.5cm (1in) oval cutter 3.5cm (1⅜in) circle cutter
- narrow spacers made from 1.5mm (¹⁄₁₆in) thick card
- cutting wheel
- piping tubes: nos 2 and 4
- dressmakers' pin
- small blossom plunger cutters (PME)

- Dresden tool
- small scissors
- craft knife
- large strawberry calyx (JEM), or similar
- dowels
- 2 piping bags
- 10cm (4in) cake card covered in pink sugarpaste (for use if top tier is sponge)
- posy pick and oasis fix
- 26g silver floristry wires
- pale pink and decorative silver ribbons and non-toxic glue stick

Stage One

♥ COVERING THE BOARD ♥

Roll out the deep pink sugarpaste and use to cover the board. Trim the edges flush with the sides of the board, taking care to keep the cut vertical. Place to one side to dry.

♥ COVERING THE CAKES ♥

1 Take the 13cm (5in) round hardboard cake board and place it under the petal cake. Place both cakes on waxed paper and cover each with buttercream or apricot glaze and marzipan, as appropriate.

2 Roll out the pale pink sugar paste and place it over the petal cake. Ease in the fullness around the sides of the cake by cupping your hand and using an upward movement (**A**). Take a smoother and smooth the top in a circular action, and then smooth around the sides ensuring the paste fits neatly into the recesses between the petals.

3 Trim away the excess paste from the base of the cake. Using a cupped hand, polish the upper edge of the petal cake to give an even finish (**B**). Leave to dry.

4 Roll out the white sugarpaste and cover the round cake; smooth and trim as before. Leave to dry.

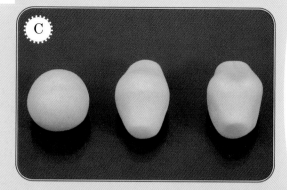

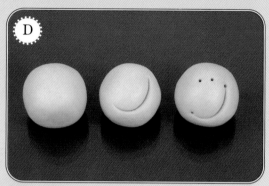

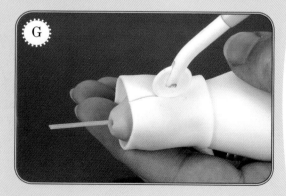

♥ THE BRIDE ♥

1 For the skirt, roll 50g (2oz) of white modelling paste into a cone, using the picture opposite as a guide. Cut the top level and place upright on waxed paper.

2 For the body, roll a marble-sized piece of flesh modelling paste into a ball. Thin the opposite sides to make a waist and neck by rolling the ball between two fingers, and then rub a finger vertically over the chest area to create a slight cleavage (**C**).

See page 53 for advice about skin-tone colourings.

3 Using sugar glue, attach the body to the top of the white cone. Insert a length of spaghetti through the neck into the skirt to secure the body in place, leaving some to give support to the head later. Leave the body to dry before dressing the figure.

4 For the head, roll 15g (½oz) of flesh modelling paste into a ball. Holding the oval cutter at 45 degrees, indent a mouth (**D**). Indent eyes with a cocktail stick and add a small ball of paste for a nose. Try using different cutters to create a variety of expressions. Leave to dry.

♥ THE GROOM ♥

1 For the shoes, take a marble-sized piece of black modelling paste and roll into a ball, divide in two and roll each half into a ball. Elongate each into a sausage shape and flatten slightly.

2 To make the trousers, take 25g (1oz) of dark grey modelling paste and roll into a 1cm (⅜in) wide sausage. Cut into two 5cm (2in) lengths, and then insert spaghetti through the length of each trouser leg (**E**). Place the shoes slightly apart on a flat surface. Vertically insert the spaghetti protruding from the trouser legs into the backs of the shoes so that the legs are standing upright. Glue in place, adjusting the position of the trousers as necessary. Glue the tops of the legs together.

A good way to roll an even 'sausage' is to use a smoother rather than your hand.

3 For the body, take 15g (½oz) of white modelling paste, and roll it into a ball and then a 3cm (1⅛in) cylinder. Glue on top of the legs and insert a piece of spaghetti into the top to hold the head at a later stage (see picture **E**). Leave to dry thoroughly in an upright position, supporting the figure if necessary.

4 Make a head as for the bride, but this time indent the smile the opposite way to the first smile to create mirror images.

Stage Two

♥ DRESSING THE BRIDE ♥

1 Use a little white vegetable fat to stop the paste sticking to the work surface while you are working with the modelling paste. To create the bodice, roll out some white modelling paste between the narrow spacers and cut into a strip, slightly wider than the height of the body. Paint sugar glue over the back of the bride and up the sides of her body. Place the strip of paste over the glue with one long edge making the lower edge of the bodice (**F**). Cut the side seams with a cutting wheel (**G**). Cut away the paste across her back to give the neckline shape. Repeat for the front of the dress. Using a no. 2 piping tube, indent buttons down the back of the bodice (**H**).

2 For the arms, roll flesh modelling paste into a thin sausage and cut into two 5.5cm (2¼in) lengths. Cut diagonally across the top of each and attach the cut area to the top of the shoulders. Squeeze the hands flat and glue them to the front of the body so that they overlap.

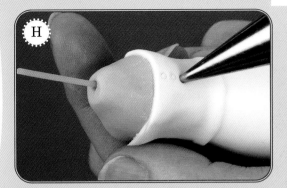

3 To create the hair, firstly make four ringlets by using your fingers to roll brown modelling paste into very thin tapered lengths. Wrap each length around a pin and leave for a few minutes (**I**). Roll out some brown modelling paste and cut out a 3.5cm (1⅜in) circle. Paint glue over the top and back of the head and position the circle of paste in place, easing in the fullness. Place a small pea-sized ball of modelling paste on top of the head and flatten slightly. Cut four 3.5cm (1⅜in) thin strips. Drape one strip over the ball with one end at the base. Using the end of a paintbrush press the strip into the centre of the ball. Attach the end of the strip to the other side of the ball. Repeat with the remaining strips (**J**).

4 Make a tiara by attaching two 4mm (⅛in) and one 6mm (¼in) dragées to the front of the bun. Attach the ringlets.

5 Add eyes by rolling very small balls of black modelling paste and placing them into the eye sockets. Add a cheek to the opposite side of the face to the smile, using a small amount of pink dust on a paintbrush. Add a small ball of modelling paste to the top of the body to create a neck, then attach the head with sugar glue.

6 For the bouquet, cut flowers from thinly rolled pink modelling paste using the plunger cutters. Place the cutter on to foam and press the plunger to release and cup the flower (**K**) and attach them on top of the hands to form a posy. Finally, stick a size 4mm (⅛in) silver dragée in the centre of each flower.

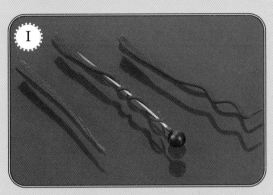

♥ **DRESSING THE GROOM** ♥

1 Roll a small ball of white modelling paste and place it on top of the groom's body to form his neck. Make a cravat from a diamond of pink modelling paste (**L**) and stick in place. Mark the fabric folds with a Dresden tool. Place a thin strip of white modelling paste around the neck and cut the ends to form the shirt collar.

2 Make a waistcoat by rolling out the grey modelling paste and cutting two 2 x 4cm (¾ x 1½in) rectangles. To create the 'V' front remove 1.5 x 1cm (⅝ x ⅜in) triangles from mirror corners (see picture **L**). Place one rectangle on the right-hand side of the body so that the 'V' shape abuts the cravat. Repeat for the second rectangle, placing it so that it slightly overlaps the front. With a pair of scissors, cut a small triangle from the lower edge of the waistcoat where the two sides overlap. Indent buttons with a no. 2 tube.

Remember that the left-hand side of the groom's waistcoat front overlaps the right side.

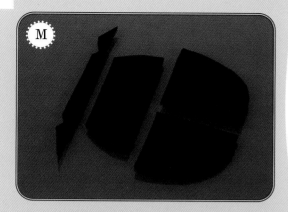

M

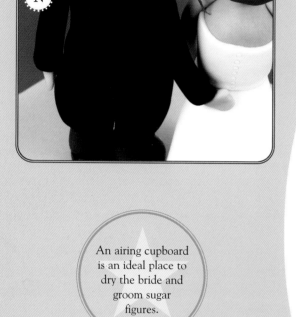

N

An airing cupboard is an ideal place to dry the bride and groom sugar figures.

3 For the tails, roll out the black modelling paste between the narrow spacers and cut out a 4 x 7cm (1½ x 2¾in) rectangle. Cut it in half lengthways, and then mirror curve two corners (M). Paint a line of glue around the sides and back of the groom's waist and arrange the two pieces in position so that they overlap at the back (N). Indent two buttons at the top using a no. 2 tube.

4 Cut a 2.25cm (⅞in) wide strip and place around the upper body above the tails. Cut the front to shape using a cutting wheel.

5 For the arms, roll two 4cm (1½in) black sausages. Open up one end of each by inserting the end of a paintbrush and gently circling. Cut diagonally across the other end, and then attach to the top of the shoulders.

6 For the hands, roll two small balls of flesh paste, thin one side to a point and flatten the other to make a hand. Form thumbs by removing a small triangle from the side of each hand. Insert the hands with the thumbs uppermost into the recesses in the arms.

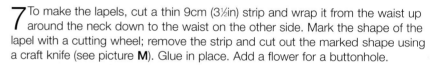

7 To make the lapels, cut a thin 9cm (3½in) strip and wrap it from the waist up around the neck down to the waist on the other side. Mark the shape of the lapel with a cutting wheel; remove the strip and cut out the marked shape using a craft knife (see picture M). Glue in place. Add a flower for a buttonhole.

8 For the hair, roll out some brown modelling paste and cut out a large strawberry calyx, or similar, and place on top of the groom's head. Add eyes and dust a cheek. Attach the head in position.

9 Place the groom next to the bride and place his right hand at the back of her waist. Allow to dry thoroughly.

♥ STACKING THE CAKES ♥

Place the base cake centrally on the prepared board. Dowel the cake, see page 16, and then place the petal cake centrally on top.

♥ DECORATING THE CAKES ♥

Place the nos 2 and 4 tubes in piping bags and half-fill each with royal icing. Use the royal icing in the piping bag fitted with the no. 4 tube to stick the heart-shaped dragées, and the bag fitted with the no. 2 tube to stick the ball dragées:

Top tier: place an upside-down heart at the base of the recess between each petal. Place one 8-10mm (⁵⁄₁₆–⅜in) silver ball either side of the heart followed by two 6mm (¼in) silver balls. Complete the row with 4mm (⅛in) silver balls. On top of the upside-down hearts vertically place two pink balls and one 4mm (⅛in) silver ball. At the outermost point of each petal stick one 8–10mm (⁵⁄₁₆–⅜in) silver ball just above the base row, and then vertically arrange above these: a silver heart, two pink balls and one 4mm (⅛in) silver.

Base tier: stick a band of upside-down heart dragées around the base of the cake. Then in the spaces between the hearts, stick a pink ball. Add another band of hearts on top of the first, and then fill the spaces with a 4mm (⅛in) silver ball and then top each with a pink ball.

♥ ADDING THE BRIDE AND GROOM ♥

If the top tier is a fruit cake: attach the figures centrally to the top of the cake using royal icing.

If the top tier is a sponge cake: attach the bride and groom to the small covered cake card. Place dowels in the cake to give additional support to the card and figures, and then attach the card centrally to the cake. Disguise the edge of the card with a ring of silver balls.

♥ FINISHING TOUCHES ♥

Insert a posy pick into the cake at the back of the couple. Hot-wire a selection of heart-shaped dragées and silver balls by heating silver wires in a naked flame until red-hot. Quickly place them on to a sugar dragée; the heat melts the sugar and so sticks them on to the wire. Paint over the blackened area of the wire with silver dust mixed with confectioners' glaze. Place a small amount of oasis fix into the posy pick to help secure the wires. Cut the wires to different lengths and place them in the posy pick. Attach the ribbons around the edge of the cake board.

If the cake is to be transported you may wish to attach the figures once the cake is in situ.

Dress it up

♥ Add one or two extra layers to the cake.

♥ Add more intricate decoration to the side of the cake, such as embroidery designs inspired by the bride's dress.

Dress it down

♥ Use a ready-made bride and groom.

♥ Replace the couple with a cluster of feathers, or make a silver and pink bead fountain topper.

Cup cakes

Cover the top of each cup cake with a disc of pink sugarpaste and decorate each with a selection of plunger flowers and silver dragées.

Exquisite Bouquet

Whether for a wedding, an anniversary, a homecoming or a special birthday, this exquisite, tiered variation of a column cake will make an impact. The delicate rosebuds are formed from flowerpaste, and detailed instructions explain how to achieve the perfect finish. The cake itself is simply covered with buttercream. Although a pink colour scheme has been used here, the colours can easily be changed to suit the occasion – you could match the colour to the fabric of a dress, for example. Silk flowers could be used, as shown in the variation.

Materials

- ♥ 1kg (2¼lb) very pale pink sugarpaste
- ♥ 600g (1lb 5oz) flowerpaste (petal/gum paste)
- ♥ paste colours: red, rose/ruby
- ♥ 3 quantities of white buttercream
- ♥ cakes: 2 x 13cm (5in) sponge cakes, each 7.5cm (3in) deep, and 2 x 20cm (8in) sponge cakes, each 7.5cm (3in) deep (see pages 8–11)
- ♥ white vegetable fat (shortening)
- ♥ sugar glue

Adapting the cake base and covering

If you would like to make the cake as a fruit cake, or you prefer sugarpaste to buttercream, cover the cakes with marzipan, if using fruit cakes, and then sugarpaste as described on page 26. Then, using a palette knife, apply either sugarpaste mixed with water until it is a piping consistency or royal icing (with 2.5ml (½ tsp) glycerine added for each egg used to make the royal icing) added in vertical strokes to the sugarpaste surface of the cake, as for the buttercreamed version.

Equipment

- ♥ boards: 30cm (12in) round cake drum (board), 20cm (8in) hardboard cake board, 2 x 13cm (5in) hardboard cake boards, 7.5cm (3in) cake card
- ♥ palette knife
- ♥ five-petal large blossom cutter (OP, cutter F6B)
- ♥ 22- or 24-gauge white floristry wires
- ♥ wire cutters
- ♥ block of polystyrene or covered oasis (floristry foam)
- ♥ 60 x 6mm (¼in) and 40 x 12mm (½in) ivory pearl beads
- ♥ jewel glue or similar non-toxic clear-drying glue
- ♥ dowels
- ♥ waxed paper
- ♥ reusable piping bag and no. 2 piping tube (tip)
- ♥ CelPad
- ♥ ball tool
- ♥ cocktail stick (toothpick)
- ♥ pink ribbon, and non-toxic glue stick

Preparation

♥ COVERING THE BOARD ♥

Roll out some of the sugarpaste and use to cover the cake drum. Trim the edges flush with the sides of the board using a small palette knife, taking care to keep the cut vertical. Place to one side to dry.

♥ ROSE CONES ♥

1 Colour the flowerpaste in a range of pinks from delicately pale through to deep pink.

2 Roll a ball of flowerpaste in your hand, and then place the edge of the top hand next to the ball; roll the ball backwards and forwards until it turns into a cone (**A**). The cone should be the same length as the width of the petals on the cutter.

Use the red paste colour as well as the ruby/rose to give warmth to the colours you mix.

A

3 Cut the white wires into thirds. Then carefully place the end of a wire into a naked flame, such as a gas burner on a cooker, or a candle. Leave the wire in the flame until it is red hot, and then quickly insert into the base of the flowerpaste cone (**B**). The heat of the wire melts the sugar, and the cone then sets securely on to the wire. Place the wired cone in the block of polystyrene or covered oasis. Repeat until you have approximately 70 cones of different shades of pink, and then leave the cones to dry out completely.

♥ WIRED PEARLS ♥

Stick the pearls on to third-length wires using jewel glue. Leave to dry in a horizontal position before placing to one side.

Stage One

♥ COVERING THE CAKE ♥

1 Level the cakes and, if using Madeira, cut away the crusts. Place the two 13cm (5in) cakes on the 13cm (5in) hardboard cake boards, securing the boards in place with buttercream. Place one 20cm (8in) cake in the centre of the prepared board and the other on the remaining hardboard. Dowel each of the cakes so that it will support the cake above (the top cake is dowelled to support the flowers, which sit on the 7.5cm (3in) cake card). Spread a thin layer of buttercream over the top of each cake and stack into the required shape.

2 Using waxed paper, draw and cut out a 30cm (12in) circle, and then remove a 20cm (8in) circle from the centre. Cut away a quarter of the circle and place the resulting collar around the base of the cake to protect the surface of the sugarpaste board.

If you are using firm cakes it may not be necessary to have as many boards and dowels.

3 Tint the white buttercream a delicately pale pink using only a very small amount of red paste colour; remember: a little goes a very long way. Adjust the consistency of the icing, if necessary: it needs to be stiff enough to go on thickly but soft enough to be applied easily.

4 Spread a thin layer of buttercream over the entire cake to seal in the crumbs. Then apply another much thicker layer with vertical strokes of a palette knife (**C**). The aim is to create a textured finish of roughly vertical stripes. Try to keep the base of the cake as neat as possible, turning the collar around as required to protect the covered board.

Experiment before applying the buttercream to the cake.

5 Place some of the remaining buttercream into the piping bag fitted with the no. 2 tube. Pipe wavy lines coming from the top of each cake at about 1.5–2cm (⅝–¾in) intervals (**D**). Remove the collar from the cake, then pipe a row of small dots around the base to neaten the appearance. Set aside to dry.

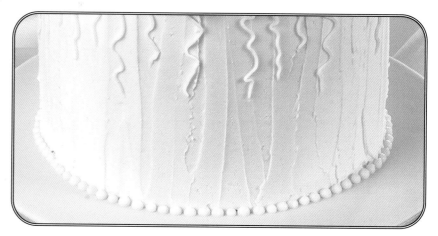

Stage Two

♥ MAKING THE ROSES ♥

Using the coloured flowerpaste, make approximately 35 bud and 35 half-roses plus a few open roses as follows:

Roses take time to make, so don't try to make them all at once; make them in stages.

♥ BUD, FIRST LAYER OF PETALS ♥

1 Smear white fat over your work board or work surface to stop the paste sticking, then, very thinly roll out one of the flowerpastes.

2 Cut out a five-petal bloom (**E**), turn it over and place it on a CelPad. Take the ball tool and stroke around the edges of each petal by pressing the tool half on the petal and half on the pad, to soften the cut edge and to frill it slightly (**F**).

The paste should be almost transparent so that you can see your work surface through it.

3 Turn the paste back over and place the centre of the blossom over one of the holes in the CelPad. Cover one of the petals (petal 1) with sugar glue, and insert the wire from one of the cones through the centre of the blossom. Take the glued petal and wrap it tightly around the cone to create a spiral, making sure that the centre of the bud is not visible (**G**).

4 Working anticlockwise, half-cover petals 3 and 5 with sugar glue. Then wrap petal 3 around the cone, making sure it stays open at the top. Tuck one edge of petal 5 underneath petal 3, and then wrap petal 5 around the cone (**H**). Finally, half-cover petals 2 and 4 with glue, and wrap around the other petals on the cone (**I**).

♥ HALF-ROSE, SECOND LAYER OF PETALS ♥

For a fuller rose add a second layer of petals. Treat the petals in the same way as for the first layer (the buds) by softening their edges with a ball tool,

then paint a line of glue along one side of each petal and in the centre. Place the wired bud through the centre of the paste as before, and then turn the whole flower upside down. Arrange the petals so that they overlap each other and stick in place. Allow the petals to harden slightly before turning upright; allow the petals to open a fraction.

♥ OPEN ROSE, THIRD LAYER OF PETALS ♥

Soften the edges of the petals as before. Using a cocktail stick, roll back two edges of each petal at an angle to the middle (**J**). Turn the paste over and cup the centre of each petal with the ball tool. Lightly paint the base of each petal with glue, then insert a half-rose through the centre, and turn the whole flower upside down. Allow the petals to fall into a natural position, and stick them in place. These petals are not overlapped and can be as open or closed as desired. Leave the flower for a few minutes then turn it upright, allowing the petals to fall open slightly; if you turn the flower too early the outer layer will flop down the stem.

The roses and pearls should be removed before cutting the cake.

♥ **ARRANGING THE ROSES AND PEARLS** ♥

Ideally, you should try to arrange your roses whilst their outer petals are still partially soft and pliable, as they will fit together more easily and are less likely to get damaged.

1 Cover the 7.5cm (3in) cake card with a dome of sugarpaste and place centrally on top of the cake.

2 Starting at the edge of the cake, insert the wire rose stems into the dome so that the roses hang halfway over the sides of the cake (**K**). Continue adding roses and clusters of pearls in sections until the top of the cake is covered. Try to arrange the roses to give an even spread of colour.

3 Roll a thick sausage of sugarpaste and place it around the base of the top column. Insert roses and pearls as for the top.

♥ **FINISHING TOUCHES** ♥

Attach the ribbon around the edge of the board using the glue stick.

Use the pearls to fill the gaps between roses.

Dress it up

♥ Add pearls to the edge of the board.

♥ Add more piped decoration to the cake itself.

♥ Add wires and or feathers to the topper.

♥ Add more tiers.

Dress it down

♥ Use shop-bought sugar flowers. Some reasonably priced sugar flowers are now available; visit your local sugarcraft shop to see what they have.

♥ Reduce the cake sizes to, say, 18cm (7in) and 10cm (4in).

Simply Stunning

For a smaller celebration use only the top column and decorate it as before. Using larger silk flowers mixed with foliage gives a very different look to the finished cake.

Templates

To use the templates, trace over them on to greaseproof paper or white paper and then transfer the template to the sugarpaste or cake as instructed in the individual projects. Carving diagrams are also included to help you carve intricate shapes from frozen cakes.

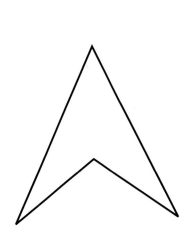

Valentine Romance (page 44)
Arrowhead template

Valentine Romance (page 44)
Hearts template

Valentine Romance (page 44)
Flight template

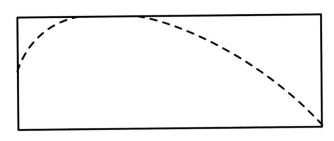

Valentine Romance (page 44)
Floral Heart (page 28)
Carving sketch

Art Deco Feathers (page 24)
Pattern template
Enlarge by 200%

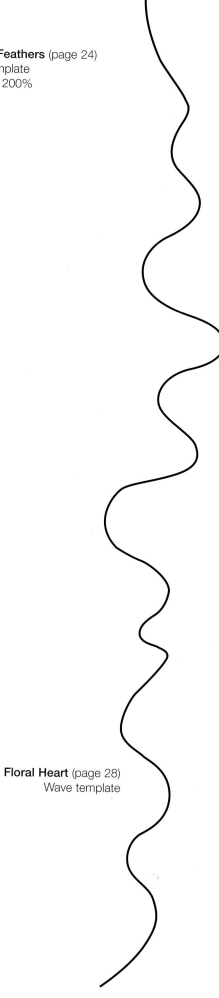

Floral Heart (page 28)
Wave template

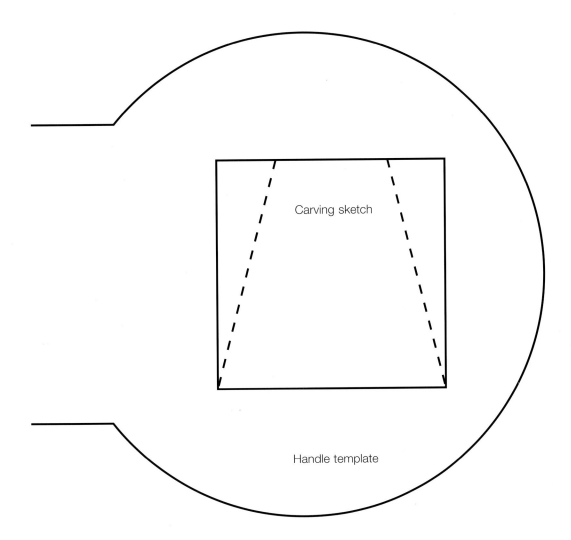

Carving sketch

Handle template

Stylish Handbag (page 32)

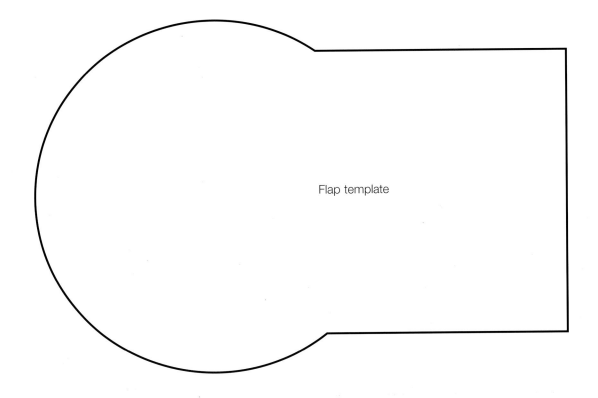

Flap template

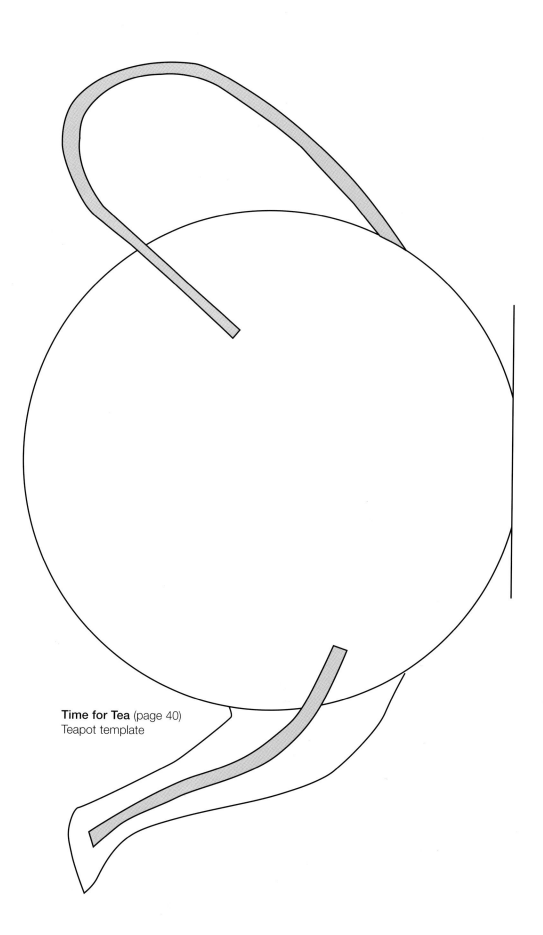

Time for Tea (page 40)
Teapot template

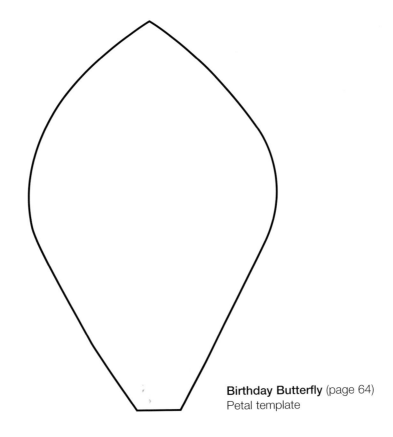

Birthday Butterfly (page 64)
Petal template

Birthday Butterfly (page 64)
Butterfly template

Acknowledgments

I would like to thank M&B for supplying me with their superb range of sugarpaste. As always, it has been great to use and has saved me hours of colouring time. I would also like to thank Patchwork Cutters for being so generous with their wonderful cutters – they are a pleasure to use.

A special thank you goes to my family, especially my mother who, having a keen and active interest in contemporary floral design, introduces me to new ideas and keeps me up to date with the latest developments in the floral world. Also my children, Charlotte and Tristan, for their honest opinions, and my sister Lucy for her valued suggestions when I needed them.

About the author

Lindy Smith is a highly experienced cake designer and author of four other cake-decorating books. This is her third book for David & Charles, her first two being *Creative Celebration Cakes* and *Storybook Cakes*.

Lindy started making cakes when her children were small and still loves the challenge of creating their unusual requests out of cake. She runs a successful cake design company called Inspirational Cakes, which produces unusual and creative wedding cakes and special anniversary cakes. She has also appeared on television, on programmes such as *The Generation Game* and presented a Sugarcraft series on *Good Food Live*. Lindy is an accredited demonstrator of the British Sugarcraft Guild and thoroughly enjoys sharing her knowledge with fellow sugarcrafters both in the UK and abroad.

For more details please visit Lindy's website: www.lindyscakes.co.uk

Suppliers

UK

Alan Silverwood Ltd
Ledsam House
Ledsam Street
Birmingham B16 8DN
tel: +44(0)121 454 3571
email: sales@alan-silverwood.co.uk
manufacturer of multisized round and spherical moulds/ball tins

Ceefor Cakes
15 Nelson Road
Leighton Buzzard
Bedfordshire LU7 8EE
tel: +44(0)12525 375237
email: info@ceeforcakes.co.uk
www.ceeforcakes.co.uk
suppliers of strong cake boxes – most sizes available

Cel Cakes (CC)
Springfield House
Gate Helmsley
York YO41 1NF
tel: +44(0)1759 371447
email: info@celcrafts.co.uk
www.celcrafts.co.uk
suppliers of a variety of sugarcraft products

FMM Sugarcraft (FMM)
Unit 5
Kings Park Industrial Estate
Primrose Hill
Kings Langley
Hertfordshire WD4 8ST
tel: +44 (0)1923 268699
email: clements@f-m-m.demon.co.uk
manufacturer of cutters

Holly Products (HP)
Holly Cottage
Hassal Green
Sandbach
Cheshire CW11 4YA
tel +44(0)1270 761403
email: june.twelves@u.genie.co.uk
www.hollyproducts.co.uk
supplier of baby head mould

Knightsbridge Bakeware Centre (W)
Chadwell Heath Lane
Romford
Essex RN6 4NP
tel: +44 (0)20 8590 5959
email: info@cakedecoration.co.uk
www.cakedecoration.co.uk
UK distributor of Wilton products

Lindy's Cakes Ltd (LC)
17 Grenville Avenue
Wendover
Bucks HP22 6AG
tel: +44(0)1296 623906
email: mailorder@lindyscakes.co.uk
www.lindyscakes.co.uk
mail-order supplier of cake separators, beads, wires, feathers and much of the equipment used in this book

M&B Specialised Confectioners Ltd
3a Millmead Estate
Mill Mead Road
London N17 9ND
tel: +44(0)20 8801 7948
email: info@mbsc.co.uk
www.mbsc.co.uk
manufacturer and supplier of sugarpaste

Patchwork Cutters (PC)
3 Raines Close
Greasby
Wirral
Merseyside CH49 2QB
tel: +44(0)151 6785053
supplier of cutters and embossers

A Piece of Cake
18–20 Upper High Street
Thame
Oxfordshire OX9 3EX
tel: +44(0)1844 213 428
email: sales@sugaricing.com
www.sugaricing.com
shop and mail-order decorating supplies

USA

Beryl's Cake Decorating and Pastry Supplies
PO Box 1584
North Springfield
VA 22151
tel: +1 800 488 2749
www.beryls.com

Country Kitchen
4621 Speedway Drive
Fort Wayne
IN 46825
tel: +1 800 497 3927 or 219482 4835
www.countrykitchensa.com

Wilton Industries, Inc. (W)
2240 West 75th Street
Woodridge
IL 60517
tel: +1 800 794 5866 (retail customer orders)
www.wilton.com

Abbreviations used in the book:	
CC	CelCakes
FMM	FMM Sugarcraft
HH	Hawthorn Hill
HP	Holly Products
JEM	Jem Cutters c.c.
LC	Lindy's Cakes Ltd
OP	Orchard Products
PC	Patchwork Cutters
PME	PME Sugarcraft
T	Tinkertech Two
W	Wilton

Index